PRENTICE-HALL FOUNDATIONS OF PHILOSOPHY SERIES

Virgil Aldrich	PHILOSOPHY OF ART
William Alston	PHILOSOPHY OF LANGUAGE
Stephen Barker	PHILOSOPHY OF MATHEMATICS
Roderick Chisholm	THEORY OF KNOWLEDGE
William Dray	PHILOSOPHY OF HISTORY
Joel Feinberg	POLITICAL PHILOSOPHY
William Frankena	ETHICS
Martin Golding	PHILOSOPHY OF LAW
Carl Hempel	PHILOSOPHY OF NATURAL SCIENCE
John Hick	PHILOSOPHY OF RELIGION
John Lenz	PHILOSOPHY OF EDUCATION
Richard Rudner	PHILOSOPHY OF SOCIAL SCIENCE
Wesley Salmon	LOGIC
Jerome Shaffer	PHILOSOPHY OF MIND
Richard Taylor	METAPHYSICS

Elizabeth and Monroe Beardsley, editor

PHILOSOPHY

OF

SOCIAL SCIENCE

FOUNDATIONS OF PHILOSOPHY SERIES

Richard S. Rudner

Washington University

PRENTICE-HALL, INC.   ENGLEWOOD CLIFFS, N. J.

PHILOSOPHY OF SOCIAL SCIENCE, Rudner

FOUNDATIONS OF PHILOSOPHY SERIES

C-66430

Current printing (last digit):
10 9 8 7 6 5 4 3 2 1

PRENTICE-HALL   INTERNATIONAL,   INC.,   London

PRENTICE-HALL OF AUSTRALIA, PTY. LTD., Sydney

PRENTICE-HALL   OF   CANADA,   LTD.,   Toronto

PRENTICE-HALL OF INDIA (PRIVATE) LTD., New Delhi

PRENTICE-HALL   OF   JAPAN,   INC.,   Tokyo

FOUNDATIONS

OF PHILOSOPHY

Many of the problems of philosophy are of such broad relevance to human concerns, and so complex in their ramifications, that they are, in one form or another, perennially present. Though in the course of time they yield in part to philosophical inquiry, they may need to be rethought by each age in the light of its broader scientific knowledge and deepened ethical and religious experience. Better solutions are found by more refined and rigorous methods. Thus, one who approaches the study of philosophy in the hope of understanding the best of what it affords will look for both fundamental issues and contemporary achievements.

Written by a group of distinguished philosophers, the Foundations of Philosophy Series aims to exhibit some of the main problems in the various fields of philosophy as they stand at the present stage of philosophical history.

While certain fields are likely to be represented in most introductory courses in philosophy, college classes differ widely in emphasis, in method of instruction, and in rate of progress. Every instructor needs freedom to change his course as his own philosophical interests, the size and makeup of his classes, and the needs of his students vary from year to year. The fifteen volumes in the Foundations of Philosophy Series—each complete in itself, but complementing the others—offer a new flexibility to the instructor, who can create his own textbook by combining several volumes as he wishes, and can choose different combinations at different times. Those volumes that are not used in an introductory course will be found valuable, along with other texts or collections of readings, for the more specialized upper-level courses.

ELIZABETH BEARDSLEY   MONROE BEARDSLEY

With love to my only parents

Louise and Max Kurz

PREFACE

In writing this brief discussion of some problems of the philosophy of social science, I have addressed those who may have a special interest in appropriate areas of philosophy, as well as those who have some technical interest in substantive problems of theory construction and validation in any of the social sciences. But it is also my intention to address those who, without being professionally involved, take an intelligent interest in the condition of contemporary social-scientific theorizing.

To those whose orientation is primarily philosophical, the book will present in brief compass some of the main problems and continuing challenges of the field. Those who are professionally concerned with the substance of one or another of the social sciences may find that the ensuing discussion sheds light on some difficulties that beset the *construction and application* of theories about social, economic, political, or psychological phenomena—phenomena that I shall use the term 'social' to describe throughout. One major aim, in fact, is to provide the student of the literature of social theory with some bases for critically assessing the variety of theoretical formulations in that literature—and indeed, to provide some tools for criticism of his own concepts and theories.

Such a student may find here means of gaining a relatively clear comprehension, not only of the character of different kinds of theoretical formulation, but of the uses to which they may appropriately be put, the scientific work, if any, that they may reasonably be expected to accomplish, and the criteria by which it may be sensible to judge their worth.

The third audience comprises those who simply wish to gain a better understanding of a segment of our civilization's intellectual product that has come to play an increasingly important role in changing our lives. This book also hopes to contribute to such understanding: negatively, by dispelling some critical misconceptions concerning the nature of social science that are prevalent even among people of advanced formal education; positively, by providing an introduction to, and an appreciation of, some fundamental things that the social scientist is doing or attempting to do.

The book's focus is upon problems of what we may call the logic or the rationale of social theorizing. However, the difficulties that infect the theoretical reaches of social science have immediate consequences for all its aspects. To show this connection is another basic aim of the book.

The book divides, roughly, into two parts. The first part is mainly an attempt to sort out and distinguish clearly several types of theoretical formulation from one another. These theoretical formulations—*theories, models, conceptual schemata, classificational systems, typologies,* and the like—figure prominently in the writings of social scientists. But there seems to be little self-consciousness about important differences among them; and the looseness with which they are treated provides fertile ground for the confusions that too frequently attend their employment. Chapter 1 offers some working tools for the analyses that follow. Chapter 2 employs some of these tools for a detailed look at the sorts of formulation just mentioned.

The second part of the book concentrates on problems attending the uses of such formulations and on various charges that the social sciences cannot use *its* formulations as the nonsocial sciences do. Chapter 3 investigates systematizing uses of *idealizations,* and also types of *explanatory* and *predictive arguments* which occur in social science. Chapter 4 considers some problems about the *complexity* of social phenomena and the *objectivity* of social inquiry.

Finally, in Chapter 5, attention is given to teleological phenomena, to the investigation of purposes and of teleological and functional systems.

My indebtedness to people whose contributions over past decades have illuminated the field for me will be obvious to anyone who has even a casual acquaintance with its literature. The roll is too long to call completely, their influence too pervasive to take account of in detail. They have included my teachers, colleagues, and students. To the students who have studied the philosophy of social science with me, in course and seminar for the past fifteen years, I am conscious of a special debt. They have passed my ideas and my mode of presenting ideas through a refining fire. In this regard, too, I owe a separate acknowledgment to my colleagues at Washington University, R. J. Ackermann, R. B. Barrett, and A. J. Stenner, who read an earlier draft of this work and whose helpful comments have made it possible to avoid many errors which would not otherwise have been avoided. In the other categories alluded to above, R. B. Braithwaite, C. W. Churchman, N. Goodman, C. G. Hempel, and E. Nagel have suggested or produced much of what is likely to be cogent in the pages that follow. Patently, they cannot be held responsible for what I have made (not hash I hope) of their teachings, suggestions, and results.

I happily acknowledge Martha Rudner's lack of character: her indefatigable willingness to be dragged to the movies at almost any moment certainly lengthened the production time of this book—but also, after all, helped make it possible.

RICHARD S. RUDNER

CONTENTS

INTRODUCTION

1

**1. The character
and scope of
philosophy of
social science** It is sometimes sensible to distinguish philosophy of social science
from other closely connected philosophical disciplines. To do so,
we need to consider two traditionally recognized types of philosophical discipline: the epistemological and the moral.

Epistemology, as a branch of philosophy, has as its quite general concern the character of knowledge and claims about knowledge.
Philosophy of science, with its focus of attention on the character of
scientific knowledge and on claims about scientific knowledge, may
conveniently be construed as a subdiscipline of epistemology. Yet,
philosophy of science too, in conformance with a much employed
rubric for the sciences themselves, may be thought of as having
its own subdisciplines: philosophy of physical science, philosophy of
biological science, philosophy of social science. (A mode of division
at least equally widespread would suggest philosophy of the natural
sciences and philosophy of the social sciences—or more disdainfully,
philosophy of the social studies. These variant modes of classifica-
tion, with their somewhat misleading suggestion that the social sciences
are not natural or are not sciences, will be avoided here for reasons to
be made clear in this and the following chapters.) But even further div-
isions of the subdisciplines of philosophy of science are not unknown in
the literature. Thus, there have been numerous treatises identified as
being on the philosophy of physics. And considerable philosophical work
has been done in areas explicitly delineated as philosophy of psychology,
philosophy of history, philosophy of economics, etc.

There is no particular need to take very seriously such classifica-
tions with their subdisciplines of subdisciplines of epistemology. Only a
fatuously obsessed taxonomist would do so. They are remarked here as
a means of indicating at once that in the discussions to follow the philosophy of social science will be construed as a discipline that takes a
middle-sized bite out of the plethora of problems confronting philoso-

phy of science; alternatively, as a discipline that takes a bite of neither the most general nor the most specific of those problems. What some of these middling general problems are will be touched on in the next section, but an inkling may be gained of this from a glance at the chapter and section titles of this book.

Philosophy of social science has, also, close connections with moral disciplines; e.g., ethics, social ethics, social philosophy, political philosophy, etc., from which, however, it may also be sensibly distinguished. If, for present purposes, we confine ourselves to examining contrasts between philosophy of social science and social philosophy, the differentiation from the moral disciplines in general will doubtless be clear enough.

Social philosophy (like its associated discipline, the history of social thought) is concerned with the varying views about the nature of desirable social systems or societies, and sometimes it puts forward its own proposals about what constitutes a good or desirable society. The assessment of the worth, as well as other characteristics, of political ideologies is a usual concern of social philosophers, as is argumentation (or sometimes merely rhetoric) in favor of the worth of one or another kind of societal arrangement or plan. Thus, Plato's *Republic* is a paradigmatic work of social philosophy and is standardly so regarded. So too are stretches of Hobbes's *Leviathan*, Locke's treatises on government, Rousseau's *Social Contract*, and voluminous writings of Marxist and non-Marxist socialists and nonsocialists, down to our own epoch.

It would be, as we shall see, most superficial to distinguish this imposing bulk of the literature of social philosophy from the slimmer body of work in philosophy of social science by pegging the distinction solely on the *normative* character of the former writings as opposed to the ethically neutral character of the latter. In the first place, very few works of social philosophy (on any reasonable definition) are unrelievedly normative in character—i.e., few do not have something to say directly or by strong suggestion about methodological problems of the social sciences; and, conversely, very few works in the philosophy of social science are unrelievedly neutral or methodological in character— i.e., do not have something to say directly or by strong suggestion about the worth of some social arrangements. In the second place, 'normative' itself is not the clearest term to come to us down the philosophical pike. Until the term is clarified, relegation of disciplines to normative or non-normative categories might prudently be regarded as tentative. Since no such definitive clarification will even be attempted in what follows, our reliance on such a term to help us distinguish social philosophy from philosophy of social science must be correspondingly qualified.

We can say in general, though, that any adequate analysis or clarification of 'normative' would have the consequence that it would be correct to call the works we have been classifying as social philosophy *more overtly normative* than the works that are typical of the philosophy of social science. For there is enough prior standardization of the term to establish this stricture as at least one of the conditions for the adequacy of any candidate clarification.

Fortunately, we do not have to depend solely on this slender reed to effect the wanted discrimination. Quite apart from normative or non-normative considerations, the differences in the problems of chief concern to the respective philosophical inquiries are sufficient to accomplish this. The problems of social philosophy are substantive ones relating to what specific views about the nature of society, and the nature of worthwhile societies, can be constructed or defended. The problems of chief concern to philosophy of social science, on the other hand, are *methodological* ones (see section 3).

The philosopher of social science is engaged not with the substance of any social theory nor with a view of what makes a good society, but with the logic of any theory construction in social science and with the logic of justification of (any) social-science theory. Where the social philosopher is concerned with the *tenability* of some one or another theory of social phenomena, the philosopher of science is concerned with the scientific *testability* of such theories. Testability is a necessary but not a sufficient condition of tenability. To go beyond concern with testability in the direction of ascertaining the tenability of a theory of social phenomena would be for the philosopher of social science to enter the domain of the social scientist or the social philosopher.

Thus, the philosopher of social science is distinguished from the social philosopher and is ranged with the (unrestricted) philosopher of science in that both focus their attention on problems of methodology. On the other hand, whereas the (unrestricted) philosopher of science bites off great or generally pervasive problems such as the construction of a theory of probability or a logic of induction applicable to all science, the philosopher of social science takes somewhat smaller or less general portions of the methodological cake—methodological problems that arise in social science with some special point or poignance, problems like the ones to be dealt with in this book.

2. A brief note on 'social science'   During the past several years, the use of the term 'behavioral science' and its cognates has enjoyed a well-deserved vogue among those who are interested in just the disciplines with which we are to be concerned. The use of 'behavioral science' has, indeed an advantage over the use of 'social science': those who wish to exclude "social" phenomena as a concern of psychology are not made uncomfortable by the appropriately neutral 'behavioral science,' embracing the psychological and social disciplines. 'Social science' may be a misleading designation in this respect. In fact, use of the term 'behavioral science' may have an additional advantage: that of not carrying so strongly the suggestion that the phenomena studied in the subsumed disciplines are limited to characteristics of sentient organisms. One of the lessons of recent conceptual and scientific advances is that the behavior of nonorganic adaptive machines of a variety of types is of keen interest to investigators of social or psychological phenomena.

Still, 'behavioral science' as a generic term to replace 'social science' has some defects corresponding to its virtues. It, too, is likely to convey erroneous suggestions. It suggests an application at once too narrow and too wide: too narrow insofar as it suggests that psychologists or social scientists may not have things other than behavior in their range of interests, and too wide insofar as a good deal of behavior of physical as well as organic entities will be of no particular interest to social scientists or psychologists.

Of course, it would be possible to redefine 'behavior' so that all and only those phenomena studied by psychologists and social scientists constituted behavior. But an obvious variant of this device is equally open to users of 'social science'—and, indeed, has already been employed in just that tradition of usage which extends the designation 'social science' to psychology. In the succeeding sections we shall follow this latter practice (as, in fact, we have in the first section). The point of the present discussion has been to obviate some difficulties that might have arisen from unreflective or unqualified uses of the term 'social science.' These difficulties should be surmounted by the understanding that now exists between us: the subject matter of psychology as well as all adaptively behaving or purposively behaving (see Chapter 5) systems of entities that may not be sentient may come within the purview of social science.

3. Some working distinctions   We have been discussing matters of terminology. These, though an important indicator of scope, do not bring us to grips with the main problems to be dealt with. For that, we must use certain concepts or distinctions, tools that have been fashioned mainly in contemporary philosophy of science. They will, in fact, be employed so crucially in what follows that an understanding of them is a precondition to making very much sense of it. It will be helpful to emphasize the working distinctions between:

(*a*) method and techniques; (*b*) the context of discovery and the context of justification (or validation); (*c*) science as process and science as product.

a) *Scientific method and scientific techniques.* The claim has often been made in the past that the social sciences are radically different from other sciences because their pursuit requires a "methodology" radically different from that required in the pursuit of other sciences.[1] Too frequently, makers of this claim have done so out of a

---

[1] Although this claim appears to have been thoroughly discredited, it has recently been revived in a series of imposing arguments by philosophers who have apparently been influenced by Wittgenstein's analyses of rule-governed actions (see section 14 and bibliography for works by Winch, Oakeshott, Peters, Hayek, and Cowling).

confusion between *methodology* and *technique*—a confusion that has vitiated either the significance or the tenability of their claim.

It is of particular moment to notice that a claim about a difference in techniques between disciplines is much less fundamental than one about a difference in methodology. For example, it has often been held—and quite correctly—that specific techniques of observation, or of experimentation, or of experimental control that are applicable to phenomena of physics are inapplicable to phenomena of sociology. But it is clear that the *methodological* thesis about social phenomena amounts by no means to the trite, simple-minded assertion that sociologists cannot accelerate Cambridge dons in cyclotrons.

In general, to become aware that various scientific disciplines employ differing techniques of investigation is not to become aware of anything significant about the nature of social science. It is not even obvious that techniques in social and nonsocial sciences differ from each other more than the techniques of nonsocial sciences differ among themselves. What grounds, for instance, could be adduced to support the claim that use of a telescope in astronomy differs from the use of a one-way mirror in small-group research more than it differs from the use of a bathysphere in ichthyology?

To claim that there is a difference in *methodology* between two disciplines or two types of disciplines is, by contrast, to make a very radical claim. For the methodology of a scientific discipline is not a matter of its transient techniques but of its *logic of justification*. The method of a science *is*, indeed, the rationale on which it bases its acceptance or rejection of hypotheses or theories. Accordingly, to hold that the social sciences are methodologically distinct from the nonsocial sciences is to hold not merely (or perhaps not at all) the banal view that the social sciences employ different techniques of inquiry, but rather the startling view that the social sciences require a different logic of inquiry. To hold such a view, moreover, is to deny that all of science is characterized by a common logic of justification in its acceptance or rejection of hypotheses or theories.

Our purpose here has not been to assess the cogency of such claims (see sections 13-21 where the question of their cogency is expressly addressed); but rather to indicate the import of our working distinction between technique and methodology. This working distinction can be made clearer by also attending to a second distinction we shall have frequent occasion to employ.

b) *The context of discovery and the context of validation.* That social science is methodologically distinguished from the other sciences is a claim that falls within the area of *philosophical* interest called the context of validation, or the context of justification, in contrast to that area of *empirical* inquiry which is called the context of discovery. It is important to see that what is at issue in such claims is a thesis about logics of inquiry or methodologies rather than about techniques; it is equally important to see that problems about the methodology or the logic of scientific inquiry belong in turn to the context of validation.

No one, in fact, has demonstrated that there is or could be such a thing as a *logic* of discovery. On the other hand, a logic, or methodology of validation, of explanation, or of prediction, is precisely what is referred to when it is asserted or denied that (regardless of differences in technique of observation or experiment) the scientific method is pervasive through all the sciences or is applicable in the investigation of social as well as nonsocial phenomena.

Now, in general, the context of validation is the context of our concern when, regardless of how we have come to discover or entertain a scientific hypothesis or theory, we raise questions about accepting or rejecting it. To the context of discovery, on the other hand, belong such questions as how, in fact, one comes to latch on to good hypotheses, or what social, psychological, political, or economic conditions will conduce to thinking up fruitful hypotheses. In short, the issues or questions appropriate to the context of discovery are, themselves, substantive issues or questions in the social sciences. They are questions to be answered by the sociology, or the psychology, or the history of science rather than by the philosophy of science. How Harvey came to think of an hypothesis of the circulation of the blood is a substantive question of the history of science. What could be meant by the claim that this hypothesis has been sufficiently confirmed by the evidence amassed for it is obviously a quite different question, and one belonging to the philosophy of science.

The view that the social sciences are methodologically distinct has sometimes been fallaciously put forward by arguments that confuse not only the notions of technique and method but also the notions of discovery and validation just considered. What should be clear is that an argument about the method of social science (i.e., one that falls into the context of validation) must be incapable of being supported by any examples purporting to show that there are greater difficulties in latching on to theories or hypotheses in the social sciences, or that some social phenomenon or other is relatively inaccessible to observation or experiment. Nevertheless, the lure of just such examples has apparently often been too seductive to resist. The following type of argument, for instance, has frequently been given, and examining it will help to put us on guard against its kin while at the same time providing us with an illustration of how using the distinction works as a tool of analysis.

Suppose, then (this fallacious type of argument sometimes goes) that a Martian is suddenly deposited on earth. Suppose, moreover, that the first thing he witnesses is a social act consisting of a man, N, voting a straight Democratic ticket in an election. However well the Martian might be able to describe the purely *physical* characteristics of this event or explain it as a *physical* event, he could never *explain* or describe (so it is argued) any of its peculiarly *social* aspects; for the *meaningfulness* of the event, the very thing (it is held) that makes it a social phenomenon, would be irremediably lost to him.

The primary thing to be noted about this argument is that it confronts us with an empirical hypothesis in the sociology of science: an empirical hypothesis about the psychology of Martians—or, more generally, about the limitations of alien imaginations. The example itself hypothesizes that creatures of certain kinds of culture or background will be psychologically incapable of thinking up certain kinds of hypotheses.

Of course, there is no mass of scientific evidence that would scientifically warrant the acceptance of such a hypothesis. Indeed, the hypothesis itself is couched in concepts that cannot be made precise in terms of any extant sound body of psychological or sociological theory. But suppose one waives all such impediments to the scientific acceptability of this hypothesis about the limitations of alien imaginations. Suppose the hypothesis be accepted as true. What is important to note then is that this would at most establish an empirical result in the context of discovery. It would establish that the investigation of social phenomena by an alien is technically very difficult, or even *empirically* impossible (i.e., contrary to empirical psychological law), since aliens are not able to think up certain hypotheses. However, to infer from this hypothesis a thesis in the context of justification, namely, that the *methodology*—the logic of validation—of the social sciences must be radically distinct from the methodology of the nonsocial sciences, is simply a non sequitur.

In the light of the failure of this kind of example to support the claim of methodological distinctness for social science, the conclusion that *no* instance adduced from the context of discovery could support it is well nigh irresistible. Be that as it may, the distinction between the two contexts can be seen as itself a useful tool of analysis.[2]

c) *Science as process and science as product.* The third working tool to be considered is closely related to the other two, without precisely coinciding with either. It involves uses of the term 'science' itself. More often than not, both in ordinary discourse and in the technical discourse of science and of philosophy, the term 'science' occurs with systematic ambiguity, and frequently this is wholly innocuous. But sometimes, and indeed on all those occasions when discussion centers on the nature of science itself or when the term's use in any rigorous argument makes equivocation perilous, the conflation of two of the meanings may result in serious confusion. The two meanings of 'science' most pertinent to present considerations are easily enough distinguished; and the damage that may be consequent on their confusion can be avoided simply by the adoption of an explicit convention such as is proposed below.

The term 'science' belongs to a rather numerous class of terms, all exhibiting a similar ambiguity, remarkable enough to have been singled

[2] For an illuminating additional discussion of this tool, see pp. 7-10 in Wesley C. Salmon, *Logic* (see bibliography).

out by philosophers of language [3] and given a special name: the *process-product* ambiguity. All the terms that exhibit this ambiguity (and these include, in addition to 'science,' such otherwise disparate terms as 'harvest,' 'swim,' 'education,' 'deduction,' 'fabrication,' 'vote,' etc.) are ones which are used to refer to a certain activity or process and also to refer to an outcome, eventuation, or product of that process. In the case of 'science,' the distinction in reference is straightforward enough. On the one hand (as process term), it is used to refer to the activities or workings of scientists or scientific institutions, i.e., to experimenting, observing, reasoning, reading, organizing research projects, etc. But on the other hand, the same term is employed to refer to a result of these activities or processes, to the product of scientific activities, i.e., to a corpus of *statements* purporting to describe one or another aspect of the universe and embodying what counts as our scientific knowledge.

To understand the following chapters, it is important to distinguish between science-as-product and science-as-process. In particular, it must be noted that 'science' (as product) refers to linguistic entities only, 'science' (as process) refers to extralinguistic phenomena.

This book will, in the main, be concerned with science as product. All uses of the term 'science' or (more usually) 'social science' unless otherwise qualified should be taken to refer to the corpus of statements that comprise the product of scientific activities. Thus, we shall deal with problems emerging chiefly in connection with those logically related sets of statements that constitute the theories or other theoretical edifices of social science.

In choosing to place the main focus of attention on what are, broadly speaking, linguistic aspects of the scientific enterprise, it might be thought that we are confining our attention too narrowly or that we are restricting ourselves to a relatively trivial domain of inquiry. There is, in fact, a view as widespread as it is curious (celebrated in the indiscriminate use of the phrase 'merely verbal') that to be concerned with linguistic analyses or with logical analyses of any discourse, or with linguistic problems at all, is to overspecialize, or even trivialize, one's concerns. No doubt this disparaging view of linguistic concerns has its genesis in the conviction that very few real and pressing problems can be construed as "merely matters of language." But whatever the genesis of such a view may be, it is surely mistaken.

That this is so will, it is hoped, become abundantly clear from the entire contents of this book. Yet, even brief reflection at this point will show that it is not a tenable view. Consider the following problems:

1. Will the stockpiling of nuclear weapons by Nation A deter Nation B from initiating a nuclear attack?
2. Does the fact that an act of person S was causally determined exculpate S of moral responsibility for that act?

[3] E.g., by Max Black, *Critical Thinking*, second edition (see bibliography).

3. Does the fact that an individual's scientific activities are socially conditioned, like most of his learned behavior, entail that science cannot achieve objectivity?

Clearly, each of these problems is of sufficient magnitude or importance to belie a charge of triviality. Yet, equally clearly, each of them, without the slightest diminution in importance, can be reconstrued as a linguistic problem in the precise sense that each can be interpreted as raising some question about linguistic entities. Thus, the problem about nuclear deterrence posed in Question 1 is construed as being about a linguistic entity, when it is posed as:

1'. Do we have sufficient evidence to accept the hypothesis 'Stockpiling of nuclear weapons by Nation A will deter Nation B from initiating a nuclear attack'?

Alternatively, Question 1 can be construed as a "linguistic problem" in the fashion of:

1". Is the statement 'Stockpiling of nuclear weapons by Nation A will deter Nation B from initiating a nuclear attack' a true statement?

Obviously reconstruing 1 as 1' or 1" involves no diminution in importance of the problem; nor has any "human responsibility" or "commitment" been evaded one whit by addressing ourselves to the problem in either the form 1' or 1" rather than in the form 1. Notice that finding the answer to 1' or to 1" provides us with an answer to 1. Similar linguistic reformulations with similar consequences hold, mutatis mutandis, for 2 and 3 and may be left as an exercise to the reader.

The point of these examples is not that all linguistic problems are nontrivial, nor even that reformulating an important nonlinguistic problem as an equally important linguistic one is always a trivial procedure, for there surely are trivial linguistic problems. Moreover, it may well be the case that construing 1 as 1", while not diminishing the importance of the nontrivial linguistic problem we confront as a result, is nevertheless a trivial process in the sense that the conversion is routine and gets us "no forrader" toward a desired solution. No, the point of these examples is to demonstrate the absurdity of treating every linguistic problem contemptuously—or interpreting 'linguistic' and 'trivial' synonymously in discussions of problems. Important problems remain important even when they are easily converted into linguistic ones.

THE CONSTRUCTION

OF SOCIAL THEORY

2

4. Theory in science   The written statements and parts of statements that are the product of social-science inquiry may be referred to conveniently as "formulations." Some, but not all, of them are formulations of *theory*. We shall refer to formulations of theory as *theoretic* formulations; formulations that, like typologies, definitional schemata, classificational schemata, etc., are *not* theories we shall refer to as nontheoretic formulations. In this chapter we shall be primarily concerned with the structure of both theoretic and nontheoretic formulations, and in Chapter 3 we shall turn our attention to uses of such formulations in social science.

The *structural* characteristics of a social-science theory are precisely the same as those of any other scientific theory. And so, at the outset, we shall talk quite generally about scientific theories.

It is unnecessary to labor the point that there are few terms of the scientific lexicon whose use, both by scientists and nonscientists, has remained for so long in so anarchic a state as has the term 'theory.' Like the term 'model,' about which something will be said below, 'theory' is used in various ways—many of them inane. Uses of the term in such locutions as 'It's all right in theory but it won't work in practice' or 'That's merely a theory and not a fact' are, for example, not ones with which the present discussion will be concerned.

In this section, the term 'theory' is employed in such expressions as 'quantum theory,' or 'general relativity theory,' or 'the theory of perfect competition,' or 'Hullian learning theory'; it will be used in the sense in which we refer to thermodynamics, or classical mechanics, genetics, or the theory of games, as theories. In just this sense it is relatively easy initially to characterize theories: A *theory is a systematically related set of statements, including some lawlike generalizations, that is empirically testable.*

Now, it would be well to be wary of whatever this deceptively

10

simple characterization seems immediately to convey; it is a highly "compressed" formulation. Indeed, logically, to *unpack* it completely would be a task beyond the scope of this book. In elaborating somewhat, for our present narrow purposes, it is necessary, for example, to forego any treatment of such key terms as 'lawlike generalization' and 'empirically testable.' [1] Instead, we shall confine our attention to the apparently less provocative, but nevertheless quite pivotal, term 'systematically related.'

What is meant by saying that the statements, of a certain set of statements, are systematically related in the sense relevant to our present concerns? Almost anyone who reaches the age of reason in Western society has at least an inkling of the import of the term. We are all familiar with the view that it is not the business of science merely to collect unrelated, haphazard, disconnected bits of information; that it is an ideal of science to give an *organized* account of the universe—to connect, to fit together in relations of subsumption, the statements embodying the knowledge that has been acquired. Such organization is a necessary condition for the accomplishment of two of science's chief functions, explanation and prediction. But the sort of systematic relatedness exemplified among the statements of scientific theories is *deductive* relatedness. Accordingly, to the extent that a theory has been fully articulated in some formulation, it will achieve an *explicit* deductive development and interrelationship of the statements it encompasses. We shall use the term 'full formalization' to refer to theories that are formulated as completely articulated deductive systems.

In practice, to be sure, only a very few theories achieve full formalization, and indeed, there are reasons (e.g., see section 10) that cast doubt on whether attempts at full formalization need always be good strategy, particularly in those sciences or branches of science where our knowledge is relatively tentative and restricted and where our uncertainty about the precise meaning and "centrality" of frequently used concepts is marked. The overwhelming majority of extant scientific theories, especially theories in social science, are not at present susceptible of fruitful or easy full formalization.

For the several paragraphs preceding, the reader who has no technical knowledge of logic has been assailed by terms such as 'deductive system,' about the precise meanings of which he may have only vague notions. It is not, of course, within the province of this volume to give rigorous explications of this and certain related notions, but because such notions figure in much of the discussion below, a preliminary informal survey of their import may be helpful.

a) Formal systems. A much truncated and quite general descrip-

---

[1] Such elaboration is provided in several important works in the recent literature of philosophy of science. See bibliography for Hempel's "Deductive-Nomological vs. Statistical Explanation" and "The Theoretician's Dilemma" [16] and [15]; and Scheffler's "Prospects of a Modest Empiricism"; and Goodman's *Fact, Fiction, and Forecast.*

tion will be given in order to convey an immediate intuitive idea of *formal language systems.* This will be followed by a slightly more detailed characterization of an *axiomatic system,* and by a characterization of scientific theories as *deductive systems.*

A formal system may be construed as a kind of language. Suppose we were faced with the problem of generating a *natural language,* say, English. What would we have to know about English in order to generate it? The term 'generation,' and its cognates, is construed here in such a way that the English language would be said to be generated were we to write down (or exhibit in some other manner) every possible *permissible* (i.e., grammatically correct) English sentence. Correspondingly, the language is said to be *generateable* when a method is produced by which it is shown that the language can be generated.

The problem thus becomes: What must we know about English in order to be able to write down each grammatically correct English sentence? Assuming this is a completeable task, a little reflection will show that we must know at least two things: the elements of the English language (i.e., the words in the total English vocabulary), and the *rules* governing permissible combinations and permutations of these elements (i.e., the complete syntax or grammar of English in accordance with which we combine words into sentences). In short, we would have to have available at least two lists, one comprising every English word, and one comprising every rule of English grammar. The language might then be generated by the routinely simple exercise of appropriately applying the items on the list of rules to permutations of items on the list of words. Indeed, we can imagine an energetic entity of rather low intelligence but vast patience, say, a high-speed digital computer, checking each possible permutation against the list of rules in its "memory," and then reading out the results of its check into one or another of two heaps—one labeled 'English sentences,' the other, marked 'non-English' (or perhaps, 'not-sentences-of-English').

It is clear that in speaking about English in this fashion, or for that matter, about any natural language, we have been taking extravagant liberties. We have made some extremely dubious assumptions, among them, that there is a class of terms that may be said to be *the* vocabulary of English, and that there is a class of rules that may be said to be *the* syntax of English. Actually, we have good evidence that both these assumptions are false; the vocabulary and rules of a natural language are obviously in constant flux.

Nonetheless, we have begun by referring to a natural language in order to emphasize the point that the two assumptions just mentioned are not dubious when made for *constructed* or artificial languages, languages in which the vocabulary and syntax can be determinately specified—and also, in order to emphasize that in this respect the generation of a constructed language *can* proceed along the lines described. The reason for this emphasis is that scientific theories are to be construed as artificial or constructed language systems, not as natural language systems.

Another fact that these preliminary remarks about natural languages serve to highlight: You will have noted that at no point in the discussion of generation procedures for natural (or constructed) languages was reference made to the *meanings* of the words that are the elements of languages. And it is indeed the case that if a list of the elements of a language, as well as a list of its grammatical rules, is available (note that the rules for English may themselves be couched in another language, say, French, so that we do not have to understand English to understand the grammar of English), then the language may be generated *without knowledge of, or without taking into account, the meaning of any word of the language.*

This important fact enables us to distinguish between *purely formal systems* and *interpreted systems.*

A purely formal system is a generated, or generateable, language to whose elements meanings are unassigned—or whose meanings, if these expressions should antecedently happen to have meanings, are deliberately disregarded. We shall have more to say about this aspect of purely formal language systems when we consider interpretations of such systems. First, however, we must take note of some structural features of constructed language systems.

Each constructed or artificial language system, as we have noted, has at least a set of *elements* (its "vocabulary") and a set of rules (its syntax or "grammar"). The syntactical rules of the system determine whether any element or permutation of elements constitutes a permissible, or "properly formulated" or "well-formulated," concatenation of those elements (e.g., a "sentence" of that system). The rules of syntax on which this determination is based are called the language's *formation rules.*

Consider the class of all permutations of some set of elements of a language we shall call '*L*.' The *formation rules* of *L* divide the class of all possible permutations into two mutually exclusive subclasses, one of which will comprise all of the grammatically permissible or well-formed formulations (for short, '*wffs*') of *L*. The other subclass will comprise the expressions which, though made up of elements of *L*, are nevertheless not grammatically correct expressions of *L*—and in this specific sense do not belong to *L*. Thus, for example, the expression 'For a the on elephant,' while a concatenation of elements (words) of English, nevertheless does not belong to the English language in the specific sense that it does not constitute a well-formed sentence of English.

We note, then, that every constructed language has at least the following sets of components:

1. elements
2. formation rules determining the class of *wffs* of the language

In addition, most languages have something we have not yet mentioned:

3. A set of definitions

b) *Definitions.* Some inkling of the character of definitions may be acquired by again turning our attention to the elements of English. If we had a list constituting the English vocabulary we might note that certain expressions (i.e., words or phrases) on it were synonyms of other expressions on it. Suppose we singled out each of these synonymous groups—that is, all groups which are such that every member of each group is synonymous with every other member of that particular group. We would then have distinguished a sublist of "internally synonymous" groups of English terms.

Now if we reflect on such groups of synonyms we can see that they indicate a certain kind of redundancy in the English vocabulary. This redundancy might be roughly expressed in the claim that if the elements of English were *reduced* by all but one member of each of the distinguishable groups of synonyms, the *assertorial power* of English would not be reduced. To put it another way, synonyms allow us to make some assertions in alternative ways but do not allow us to make *additional* assertions. By the same token, discarding the synonyms of a term does not deprive us of the capacity to make assertions we could hitherto have made in that language.

The dispensability-in-principle of a synonym, however, does not mean that it is either necessary or desirable to omit it from a language's list of elements. (On the contrary, we shall see that it is usually desirable, for a variety of reasons, to keep the list redundant.) Still, the possibility of this sort of redundancy enables us to regard the *total* vocabulary of a language as divisible into two mutually exclusive sublists, one of which (the list of *primitive,* or *undefined,* elements of the language) will contain (*a*) all terms that have no synonym at all in the list, and (*b*) at most, one element from each of the internally synonymous groups. The second sublist will then contain the remaining elements, i.e., the *defined* terms of the language; every member of this list is a synonym of some member or members of the sublist of primitive elements.

The ways in which the natural language of a given language community is learned and used are not yet wholly understood by social scientists; as a consequence, our confidence in being able to explicate 'synonymy,' or 'sameness of meaning,' or even in being able to delimit the language's internally synonymous groups, must be restrained. But when we turn from natural to artificial or constructed languages, we become more thoroughly the masters, so to speak, of the situation.[2]

In a *constructed* language, synonymies are established through *explicit* definitions, each of which is itself a rule of the language's syntax (a rule determining permissible replaceability of some term in contexts of the language). We shall explore the ramifications of definitional rules more thoroughly below. For the present, it will suffice to note

---

[2] Masters in a way in which Humpty Dumpty, speaking English, *really* couldn't be. And *there's* glory for you!

some salient features of definitions. First, the totality of elements of a given language system could be defined in that system only on pain of absurdity, as is obvious from the fact that a definition signalizes the redundancy or eliminability of a term; and to define all the terms of a system would be to declare all its elements at once redundant. It is also obvious that to define all the elements of a system would lead to vicious circularity in definition; for every definition of a system defines some term of the system "by" some other term of the system. Accordingly, if all elements of a system were defined, they would be defined in terms of each other. Second, though it is the case that some term or other must be primitive or undefined in any constructed language system, it would be fallacious to conclude from this that any term is *undefinable*. For any given term it is always in principle possible to construct a language system in which it occurs as a defined term of that system.

Let us, for the time being, leave this preliminary scrutiny of the definitional component of constructed language systems and return to our examination of such systems in general. We have seen that any such system L comprises the totality of its *wffs* as determined by application of its syntactical rules of formation to its elements. The system thus characterized, however, is not an *axiomatic system* and, as we shall see, not a *deductive system*.

c) *Axiomatic systems.* In order to construct an *axiomatic* system in L at least two further conditions must be fulfilled: (1) we must make a selection of a subset of *wffs* from the totality of *wffs* in L and designate them *axioms*. And (2) we must formulate a group of syntactical rules called *transformation rules*, such that application of these to the axioms results in the derivation of some (but not all) of the remaining *wffs* of L. Wffs thus derivable are called *theorems*.

Thus, an axiom system C is always a subsystem of some language L. C may consist of a selection of *wffs* of L which, relative to syntactical rules of transformation, are *underived* (hence, are axioms of C), and from which, by application of those transformation rules that are derivation rules, certain *wffs* of L are derivable (and hence, are theorems of C).

It follows that the *total* syntax of a language containing an axiom system will be comprised of at least three kinds of syntactical rules: (*a*) rules of formation, which determine the *wffs* (or permissible expressions) of the language, (*b*) rules of definition, which distinguish primitive from defined elements of the system and which establish permissible replacement or transformations on *wffs*, and (*c*) transformation rules, which determine which derivations of *wffs* from an initially selected set of *wffs* are permissible.

The significance of calling definitions *rules of replacement* may be illuminated if we think of some definition from a suitably precise subportion of English. Thus, in English a definition of the term 'vixen' is given by 'female fox.' We may indicate this definition by adopting a useful convention of notation.

'vixen' $=_{df}$ 'female fox'

The term left of the definitional sign, i.e., the term being defined, is called the *definiendum*. The term right of the sign—the term doing the defining—is called the *definiens*. Now, given this definition, to construe it as a rule of replacement is to enable reference to it in justifying certain changes or transformations we might make in contexts of discourse in English. Thus, if we employed or confronted a context like

1. The hounds hunted the vixen,

we could, on the basis of (i.e., with the justification provided by) our definition, *replace* the term 'vixen' by the term 'female fox,' thus transforming the context into

2. The hounds hunted the female fox.

It is important to notice that transformations based on definitional replacements always preserve the *truth-value* (i.e., the truth or the falsity) of contexts in which such replacements are made. This is to say that if Sentence 1 is true, it will remain true after the definitional replacement that transforms it into 2. Similarly, if 1 is false, so, too, will be its transform, 2. Definitional replacement does not turn a true sentence into a false one nor a false one into a true one; it *preserves* whatever truth-value originally obtained.

A little reflection on what we have just been illustrating will show that the rules of definition are, in fact, one species of transformation rule; and indeed, in practice they are usually assimilated to the list of the axiomatic system's transformation rules with the result that the total syntax of L is usually construed as consisting of just two types of syntactical rule: formation and transformation.

Again, in practice, when attention is focused on axiomatic development (i.e., on the construction and elaboration of some axiomatic system), one proceeds by listing a set of primitive elements, a set of formation rules, a set of axioms, and a set of transformation rules, all of which, taken together, determine the axiomatic system. The system is developed by deriving theorems, and by introducing new elements through the addition of definitional rules to the set of transformation rules.

At this point, the reader should recollect that the artificial systems we have been dealing with thus far are purely formal, or *uninterpreted*, constructed systems, i.e., systems whose elements have not been assigned meanings. A purely formal, or uninterpreted, axiomatic system is called a *calculus*. It is important to note that the entire process of generating a calculus may be accomplished *purely syntactically*, that is, without recourse to the meanings (or *semantical* characteristics) of any expression in the system. Understanding the significance of this remark puts us in a position to understand more adequately the concept of a *deductive* system. Accordingly, let us begin by considering some of the things involved in *interpreting* a purely formal system.

d) Interpretation of formal systems. Suppose that one of the axioms of our purely formal system or calculus, C, looks like the following.

$$1. \quad aO(bOc) = (aOb)Oc$$

These symbols, as they originally appear in the calculus, are uninterpreted, i.e., we assign no meanings to them. But now, suppose by formulating an additional series of rules, to be called *rules of interpretation*, we make explicit the convention that the lower case letters are to be construed as numerical variables, that '0' is to indicate the mathematical operation of summation, that '=' is to be construed as mathematical equivalence, and finally, that parentheses are to punctuate or indicate the *scope* of the operators. If we adopted conventions or rules of interpretation such as those just described, the resulting interpreted expression would be a familiar truth of elementary algebra of arithmetic; namely, the one ordinarily written as follows.

$$1'. \quad x + (y + z) = (x + y) + z$$

Axiom 1 is from the purely formal system generally referred to as abstract Boolean algebra.

Purely formal systems like abstract Boolean algebra—ones that are determined by a set of syntactical rules—have no meaning in the precise and literal sense we have been delineating. Nevertheless, interpreted or *applied* linguistic systems always do have meaning. Such systems not only have syntactical rules but also certain additional rules, called semantical rules of interpretation, which explicitly confer meaning on the expressions of the system by indicating what the elements of the system are to designate. Semantical rules also determine the conditions of truth or falsity for the combinations of expressions of the system that comprise its sentences.

Providing an interpretation for a purely formal system or calculus by supplementing its syntactical rules with semantical rules is still not sufficient to give us the notions we require wholly to clarify the deductive structure of a scientific theory. We mentioned early in this section that a scientific theory was a set of systematically related statements, and that the kind of systematic relatedness involved among those statements was *deductive*—that, in short, a scientific theory constituted a *deductive system*. But a calculus is not a deductive system, and it doesn't automatically become a deductive system when it is interpreted. It must fulfill certain other conditions, which it would be beyond the province of this book to elucidate in detail, but which, if fulfilled, would guarantee the following.

*For each possible interpretation of the calculus (by semantical rules)
that makes the axioms true, every theorem (that is, every wff derivable
from the axioms in the calculus by applications of the transformation
rules) likewise is true.*

We shall reserve the term 'calculus' for uninterpreted axiomatic
systems, and the term 'deductive system' for interpretations of calculi
that fulfill the condition alluded to above. The term 'purely formal
language' will be employed only to refer to uninterpreted languages, and
the term 'purely formal system,' to any uninterpreted system.

The reader who has followed this informal and highly truncated
account of the nature of a deductive system should now be in a position
to understand better our characterization of a scientific theory as a
deductively related set of statements. He should, moreover, have a better
idea of what is involved in a full formation of a theory as a completely
articulated system. A theory thus articulated will, for example, provide
an explicit delineation of its primitives, rules, axioms, and deductions.

Before turning our attention from full formalizations of scientific
theories to formulations of other kinds of theoretical structures, it may
be well to guard against a misconception which might be occasioned by
the foregoing account. It would be a serious mistake to construe the
foregoing account as a description of the *actual* process by which theories
are, or should be, formulated. It is *not* a description of any *process* of
theory construction, actual or proposed; it is, rather, an account of the
logical or structural characteristics of theories. Specifically, it would be
a misconstrual of the aims of this section to understand it as advocating
that a scientist who wishes to formulate a theory should do so by first
constructing an artificial language system and then a calculus and then
an interpretation, etc. The association of a calculus with every theory is
not a genetic, chronological, or practical association, but a *logical* one.
Being clear about the existence and character of this logical association
is a matter of some importance for the philosopher of social science, and
sometimes for the social scientist too; but its importance here does not
entail anything about the manner of a social scientist's actual theory-
building practices.

5. The logic of concept introduction   The accretion or building of theory often requires the introduction
of new concepts (i.e., predicates—terms denoting certain char-
acteristics, or terms applicable to entities said to have certain
characteristics).[3] Thus, suppose that we have achieved some
theoretical formulation descriptive of the behavior of small, task-oriented
groups. Among the concepts that could well figure in such a formulation

[3] In this book, 'concept' and 'predicate' are intended synonymously. In particular,
use of the former is *not* intended to suggest anything extralinguistic: neither a
psychological entity like a thought, nor a platonic entity like an attribute. 'Concept'
and 'predicate' are used to apply to expressions that are often referred to as *property-
terms* as well as those often called *relation-terms*.

might be the predicates 'group member,' 'cooperative behavior of group members,' 'conflicting behavior of group members,' 'goal of a group,' and 'goal of an individual.' But suppose we wish also to *introduce* a concept, say, 'competitive behavior of group members,' whose intended range of application is not identical with any single, hitherto occurring predicate in our formulations. How, precisely, is such an additional concept to be introduced? What is the logic or rationale of a mode of concept introduction?

Strictly speaking, there are only two ways in which a new concept may be introduced into a theory: by definition (i.e., defining the new term by means of terms already occurring in the theory), or by adding the new concept *as a primitive* to the theory's set of primitive terms. Again, strictly speaking, the introduction of a new concept into a theory by adding it (as a primitive) to that theory's antecedent set of primitives, is not actually to increment that theory; it is, rather, to *replace* the old theory with a new one. For one of the things that determines the identity of a theory is its set of primitives.[4] In practice, though, even relatively self-conscious theorists are likely to speak as if they are dealing with the "same" theory even after adding to its set of primitives. And as long as the strict point has been noticed, we too shall, for the most part, indulge in this practice. Thus, we will speak without further qualification of having "introduced the concept 'competitive behavior' into our theory by adding it to our theory's set of primitives."

If, on the other hand, we are able to choose the alternative, and preferable, mode of concept introduction—adding the concept by means of a definition—we should thereby, in a sense, leave the assertorial power of the theory intact.[5] We shall return to problems of selecting and incrementing sets of primitives after exploring a little further the notion of definition.

As indicated in section 4, a definition may perhaps best be understood as a syntactical or grammatical rule of linguistic usage. Technically it takes the following form:

$$\text{'. . . . .'} =_{df} \text{'- - - - -'}$$

It may be read, '. . . . .' (some term) is definitionally equivalent to '- - - - -' (some other term[s]). For example, the definition

'competitive behavior' $=_{df}$ 'conflicting behavior of a group member, which increases the probability of the attainment of a goal of the group'

would be read: 'Competitive behavior' is definitionally equivalent to

---

[4] Logically, two theories T and T' cannot be "identical" if (a) the primitives of T are wholly mutually independent (*e.g.*, there is no overlap of reference) and the primitives of T' are wholly mutually independent; and (b) the set of primitives of T is a different set (even if different by containing only one less primitive) from that of T'.

[5] Preferable because of the desirability of maximal *structural simplicity* as a characteristic of theories.

'conflicting behavior of a group member, which increases the probability of the attainment of a goal of the group.'

The term being defined, the *definiendum*, is left of the definitional equivalence sign; the *definiens* is on the right. Every term in the *definiens* will be either a primitive term or one that has been ultimately defined by (i. e., is linked by a chain of definitions to) primitive terms. That some term is definitionally equivalent to some other term specifies at least that the *definiendum* and the *definiens* are mutually replaceable in *any* statement (in the theory) without altering the truth-value of that statement. A definition amounts to the stipulation that if a statement is true it will remain true after terms in it have been replaced by definitionally equivalent terms: so too mutatis mutandis for a false statement.[6] This *salva veritate* condition is a necessary part of the significance of every explicit definition—and indeed it has been held that this is the entire significance of any assertion that a pair of terms are definitionally equivalent.

Incidentally, the existence and prima-facie cogency of the *salva veritate* condition throws doubt on the propriety with which so-called "operational definitions" and "ostensive definitions" are thought of as definitions at all. It seems evident that the processes named by these two terms are thought to be definitions simply because they are processes by which the *meanings* of terms are conveyed. But little reflection is needed to reveal that the conveyance of meaning is not a necessary, and certainly not a sufficient, condition for something to achieve the status of a definition.

It is not a *sufficient* condition, for meanings are conveyed by an immense number of things (from the tilt of an eyebrow to the tilt of a bomber's wing) which it would be absurd to refer to as 'definitions.'

That it is not *necessary* for a definition to convey meaning is evinced by the existence of the great number of definitions in purely formal mathematics and logic that do not convey meanings and that are introduced solely to serve the purpose of notational convenience.

In the light of this, 'operational definition' and 'ostensive definition' may be recognized as misnomers. The first refers to the process of conveying the meaning of a term by specifying the operations required to test for the presence of the thing to which that term refers; the second refers to the process of conveying the meaning of a term by exhibiting the things to which the term refers. It would be more accurate to label these processes 'operational *conveyance* of meaning' and '*conveyance* of meaning by ostension.'

Of course, although definitions need not convey the meanings of their *definienda*, it is patent that they sometimes do and that they are frequently constructed for the purpose of doing so.

[6] But see Goodman's illuminating discussion of this condition, and of definitions and constructed systems in general, in *The Structure of Appearance*, Chap. 1 (see bibliography).

So far we have not turned our attention to any of the criteria that might determine the selection of a set of extralogical (descriptive) primitives in a fully formalized theory. The very ubiquity of definitions in science shows that alternative choices are possible. What criteria *should* determine our choices of the concepts that will be primitive in scientific theories we construct?

One criterion is obvious and of special importance for the present discussion; namely, that sets of such primitives should be comprised of *observational,* or as we shall sometimes say, *experimental,* terms (i.e., that such predicates should refer to observable features of the universe). The import of positivist, pragmatist, and operationalist philosophies of science on the thinking of methodologically self-conscious scientists has no doubt been so pervasive as to require no extended comment here on this point. But from the foregoing discussion, it should be clear that one way of meeting the demand of experimental testability on any candidate concept that we are considering introducing into a theory is to introduce it through definition by primitives which, themselves, *are known to have experimentally testable reference.* Thus, an important by-product of the experimental-testability criterion for a set of primitives lies in the fact that any set that meets this condition in a theory guarantees that all new concepts introduced through definition will, in turn, be experimentally testable concepts.

The attempt to meet the criterion of experimental testability or observability for a theory's extralogical primitives is a recognized inheritance of the classical empiricist philosophies that have been associated with the rise of modern science. In recent years, however, scientists and philosophers of science have come to realize that the unqualified fullfillment of this requirement is immensely difficult, and perhaps impossible, and that insistence on its fullfilment for the validation of theory may be an unjustifiable demand.

The occurrence of two sorts of concept and the apparent unavoidability of introducing them into any empirical theory of significant explanatory or predictive power have revealed serious difficulties in the way of meeting the traditional empiricist demands embodied in the criterion of testability. These two sorts of concept are generally referred to as *dispositional* and *theoretical.*

A vast and swiftly growing literature devoted to the notorious recalcitrance of these concepts (see bibliography for Hempel's "The Logic of Functional Analysis," which has a bibliographic list) attests to the complexity, as well as to the philosophical profundity, of many of the issues involved. Consider, first, dispositional predicates. Clearly, the claim that some entity has a disposition to manifest, or potentiality for manifesting, some property, is different from the claim that it *is* manifesting that property. Thus, to say of a house that it is *combustible* is obviously not the same as saying it is *burning.* It is, of course, possible that entities that have dispositions to manifest certain properties may *never* exhibit those properties. A lump of sugar that we *truly* assert is *soluble* may never (and for the assertion to be true, need never) *dissolve;* instead, it may be vaporized in an atomic test explosion or burned to ashes in a fire. Now, the ubiquity and the pivotal character of such dispositional predicates in all branches of empirical science is patent not only in the frequency of occurrence of "ible," "uble," and "able" terms like 'combustible,' 'soluble,' 'observable,' etc., that, so to speak, wear their dispositionality on their sleeves, but also when we consider the very large number of other terms, like 'magnetic,' 'elastic,' 'attitude,' 'reflex,' 'habit,' 'response repertoire,' 'personality,' 'hardness,' 'conductor,' etc., that, under analysis, turn out to be dispositional predicates. A glance at even this minuscule list is sufficient to indicate the essential role of dispositional predicates in the theories of contemporary science.

The difficulties presented by these terms have been felt to lie in the fact that they themselves (since they are taken not to refer to observable features of the world) do not meet the criterion of testability or observability for sets of primitives, and hence, according to that criterion, should not be introduced into a theory as primitives. At the same time, no methodology to automatically assure their adequate definability *by* observational primitives is known—or seems likely to be forthcoming—so that their blanket introduction into a theory acceptable to traditional empiricism by means of definitions seems equally barred.[7]

A second suggestion that has advanced our understanding of the issues is the proposal that we modify the traditional empiricist criterion for the clarity of concepts. The suggestion, in effect, is that the meaning of some dispositionals is antecedently (to the construction of the theory) as clear to us as is the meaning of terms having direct observational reference. The inclusion of such dispositionals in a set of primitives for a scientific theory is, then, held to be empirically innocuous. This modified *clarity* criterion, it should be noted, does not countenance the blanket admissibility of all dispositionals into sets of primitives; it does counsel the piecemeal judging of each candidate on its "antecedent-clarity" merits.

Though there are some signs of progress in the assault on the problems of dispositionals, this does not ameliorate the difficulties for empiricism presented by the second kind of term mentioned above—the *theoretical.* The problems presented by theoreticals seem as formidable as ever.

---

[7] In Scheffler's "Prospects of a Modest Empiricism," and particularly Goodman's *Fact, Fiction, and Forecast,* suggestions for dealing with such terms have advanced the assault on the "problem of dispositionals." Goodman has shown how to achieve adequate definitions of some dispositionals by employing in their *definientia* not the corresponding manifest predicates, but rather, other manifest predicates (associated with those corresponding manifest predicates in well-confirmed lawlike sentences). It is clear, however, that although this suggestion advances our progress it can only be satisfactory to the degree that the concept 'lawlike sentence' is itself clear. But as Goodman has also pointed out, we are far from having a satisfactory account of 'lawlike sentence.'

Dispositionals may be roughly distinguished from theoreticals insofar as the former may be said to refer in standard cases to nonobservable or nonmanifest characteristics of observable entities while the latter refer to nonobservable or nonmanifest characteristics of *nonobservable* entities. Thus, theoreticals include terms such as 'electron,' 'superego,' 'institutional inertia,' 'cultural lag,' which do not or are not (when the appropriate theories come to be formulated) likely to apply to observable entities at all. Theoreticals also include such terms as 'length,' 'volume,' 'mass,' 'charge,' 'habit strength,' 'demand,' 'age,' and 'preference,' indeed all metrical concepts which as "variables" or functors in scientific theories include in their range some values that are not, even in principle, observationally directly discriminable.

We not only lack appropriate definitional means for introducing such terms, but also, claims for their antecedent clarity can scarcely be credited. The dilemma is a critical one, not only for philosophers of science, but for any scientist who is concerned with the scientific tenability or cogency of his theory-building efforts; significant or useful theory cannot seem to dispense with such terms, yet the empiricist heritage of science seems to proscribe their use.

It should be said at once that these problems are not peculiar to the philosophy of social science. Nevertheless, there is a sense in which their import for social science is especially exacerbated by the lesser degree of formalization of theories characteristic of the social sciences. The less we succeed in articulating a theory, the less we can be confident of the dispensability, indispensability, or in general, the "structural position" of any of its concepts. The fact that we now do, and indeed for the foreseeable future may, have to rest content in our social-science theorizing with something considerably short of full formalization, makes especially poignant the question of what is an acceptable degree of partial formalization, or how far *should* we formalize. Can we, in fact, give a relatively clear meaning to the notion of a *partial formalization*, and if so, can we provide techniques and a methodology appropriate for partial formalization? We shall examine these questions and their possible answers after we have considered some theoretical formulations, other than theories, that occur in social science.

6. Models   The terms 'model' and 'theory' share a melancholy lack of uniformity in the vocabularies of scientists and others who talk about science. Sometimes the two are employed simply as synonyms; sometimes 'model' is used to refer to *any* theoretical formulation other than a theory. There is one established usage in the formal sciences (logic and mathematics) where the term refers to extralinguistic entities—those in the extension of a distinguished interpretation of some calculus, e.g., the natural numbers (as opposed to the theory of natural numbers).

The usage we shall adopt here is none of these, though it appears to be employed in empirical science at least as frequently as any of them;

and it shares with the usage of 'model' in formal science an amenability to precise and relatively simple explication.[8]

According to this usage, then, *a model for a theory* consists of an alternative interpretation of the same calculus of which the theory itself is an interpretation.

Suppose, for example, that we have formulated both a theory of personality and its underlying calculus. Moreover, suppose that the theory is a version of the *humors* theory of personality (a manageable example of a theory that enjoyed a certain vogue some years ago). Our theory hypothesizes that certain personality states at any given time are functions of the quantitatively determined proportions among, say, four different body fluids (e.g., blood, bile, etc.). To claim this is to hold at least that there is some empirical law that assigns or connects a specified personality state at a given time to specified proportions of the four fluids present in the body at that time. Suppose, finally, that our calculus C, of which our theory T is an interpretation, has a logical set of rules, that four of its axioms are interpreted as empirical laws, and that six of its primitives are interpreted in T as descriptive predicates. The remainder of its axioms and primitives would be interpreted as analytic statements (i.e., truths of logic or mathematics) and logical (or mathematical) elements. Each of the axioms and theorems of our articulated humors theory of personality T has its counterpart in some axiom of the abstract, uninterpreted calculus C, and the meaning of each axiom of T is determined by the assignment of meanings to the primitives (which are the constituents of each axiom) through use of a set of semantical rules of interpretation S. What has just been described, then, exemplifies the structural characteristics of theories already outlined in section 5.

But our theory T is only one of the indefinitely large number of possible interpretations of C. Suppose that, instead of employing the set of semantical rules S (which rules, you will remember, interpret the calculus' primitive "abstract" signs as the (observational) predicates 'blood,' 'phlegm,' 'bile,' etc.), we employed the quite different set S' (where S' takes the same abstract signs of the calculus and interprets them as *paint-pigment* predicates such as 'red pigment,' 'green pigment,' 'black pigment,' etc.). The resulting theory would *not* be about personality states as determined by proportions of body fluids, but say, about the color states of batches of pigment that have as constituents variously colored pigments in various proportions (e.g., "twice as much red pigment as blue pigment," etc.). We would thus have a second interpretation of the same calculus.

Two different interpretations of the same calculus may be diagrammed as follows.

[8] For a lucid explication of 'model' see Braithwaite's *Scientific Explanation,* to which the above explication is chiefly indebted. For an equally lucid account of this and other uses of the term see Brodbeck's "Models, Meaning, and Theories." (Both are listed in the bibliography.)

$C\begin{cases}\text{becomes by Semantical} \\ \text{rules } S \text{ of interpretation}\end{cases} T$	$C\begin{cases}\text{becomes by Semantical} \\ \text{rules } S' \text{ of interpretation}\end{cases} M$	
Axioms	*Axioms*	*Axioms*
1	A1	A1′
2	A2	A2′
.	.	.
.	.	.
.	.	.
n	An	An′

Theorems	*Theorems*	*Theorems*
Th.1	Th.1	Th.1′
Th.2	Th.2	Th.2′
.	.	.
.	.	.
.	.	.
Th.n	Th.n	Th.n′

In such a situation (i.e., one in which two different deductive systems are both interpretations of the same underlying calculus), we say that the two interpreted theories are *isomorphic*. One of such a pair of isomorphic theories may be regarded as being a model of, or furnishing a model for, the other. Which is regarded as the model, and which the theory of primary concern, will not depend on any structural feature of the two theories, but merely on which subject matter we are primarily interested in. Thus, if we are primarily interested in personality, we take M, the theory of pigments, to be a model for T. If, however, we are primarily interested in pigments or color states, we take T to be a model for M.

A calculus C may be susceptible both to *empirical* and *analytic* interpretations. An interpretation is analytic if *all* of the axioms of C become truths of logic or mathematics on that interpretation. An interpretation of C is empirical if at least one of its axioms on that interpretation is nonanalytic (i.e., empirically disconfirmable). Accordingly, an empirical theory may have either an empirical model or a mathematical (or logical) one.

Why should a scientist ever concern himself with a model? In one rather obvious sense, the point of employing a model belongs to the context of discovery rather than to that of validation; for models function as heuristic devices in science. If, for whatever reason, we find it difficult or uncongenial to think about, or to work with hypotheses about, blood, phlegm, or bile, etc., we may, instead, think about or work with an isomorphic set of statements about color pigments. We may *work* with the latter, even though our primary concern is personality, because we find it *easier* either to effect error-free deductions from the axioms or to think of a greater number of possible theorems that can then be checked to ascertain whether they *do* follow in the model. Again, the sheer familiarity or concreteness of an empirical model, in contrast with the unfamiliarity or intangibility of the subject matter of the theory of primary concern, may be the chief factor that leads us to employ that model. Thus, to take another example, a theory of the flow of water through pipes might be employed as a model for a theory of electric current in wires. Working in terms of the familiar subject matter of the model, its user need only make the most routine translations into the theory of concern after he has arrived at desired results in the model.

The heuristic efficacy of *empirical* models stems, no doubt, from the greater familiarity or ease of visualization of their subject matters. The efficacy of most *mathematical* models, however, stems from the fact that a great number of mathematical theories have already achieved extensive deductive elaboration. When one of these mathematical theories (e.g., the system, or theory, of real numbers) is isomorphic with an empirical theory (e.g., a theory involving operations of measurement on mass), a vast stock of *already proven theorems* is immediately available to the scientist from the mathematical model for translation into the empirical theory.[9] Indeed, all theories of social science in which metrical concepts occur, all that encompass so-called "measurable concepts," employ such models or are deductively manipulated, mainly through the intervention of some translation, from one or another mathematical or logical model.

Very little reflection is required to realize that use of either empirical or analytic models may be enormously valuable heuristically. Nevertheless, their use is also fraught with certain dangers, and the concomitant risks are serious. This is especially true in those areas where, as in most social-science formulations of theory, one has only a sketchy idea of the logical structure of the empirical theory of concern. Obviously, one's confidence that a given (mathematical or empirical) theory is isomorphic to—has the same logical structure as—the theory of primary concern, must be qualified to the extent that one is ignorant of the logical structure of the theory of primary concern. To translate from the theorems of some system that we are guessing to be a model, in the face of such ignorance, is to risk attributing to our theory of concern implications that, quite literally, our theory does not have. This peril is present just as long as the required isomorphism between model and theory remains *undemonstrated*. The great frequency with which this risk is run in the social sciences is wholly out of line with its quite considerable seriousness.

Related to this general danger, which is associated both with the employment of empirical and analytic models, are some difficulties peculiar to an unwary use of each of the two types. When we use an empirical model, like the hydraulic model for electric current flow, or

---

[9] In most areas of science the scientist accomplishes such translation routinely and unselfconsciously—"calculating directly with numerals" he is scarcely aware of the translations to and from theory and mathematical model. But like M. Jourdain's unawareness of his skill at prose, the scientist's unawareness of *his* prowess at translation does not alter the fact (i.e., the existence of the logical relationships between model and theory) that justifies exercise of this power.

the pigment-mixture model for the humors theory of personality, our knowledge of the kinds of entities to which the model itself applies will often by no means be exhausted by the axioms and theorems of which the model is comprised. Thus, we know very much more about water than merely how it behaves in conduits; and we know much more about various pigments than about the colors they yield in certain combinations. But in employing the water-conduit theory or the pigment-mixing theory as models, it would be quite unjustified to translate any information not actually deducible in those models into the theory of concern, no matter how familiar with, or how confident of, this extrinsic information we might be. To take a final example of this point, if we are employing some theory about body-temperature homeostasis in whales as a model for a theory about some homeostatic characteristic of modern political states, it would be fallacious to translate our *extrinsic* knowledge of the way in which whales care for their young into any corresponding hypothesis about the way in which modern states deal with their colonies (no matter how well-confirmed our knowledge of, say, suckling behavior of whales may be).

These examples show that the relation of model to theory of concern is at once more precise and circumscribed than is the looser relationship of *analogy* which we might find to hold between two different subject matters. When the model relationship does obtain, we are, so to speak, guaranteed that implications of the model have corresponding implications in the theory of concern. But this guarantee extends only to implications *in the model* and not to any exterior knowledge of the model's subject matter. On the other hand, when we attempt to exploit heuristically a noted analogy between different subject matters, we have no guarantee that any given statement about the subject matter of the analogue will have a counterpart translation in the theory of concern, though by the same token, our translational attempts are not logically restricted to any one theory of the analogue subject matter.

The fallacy of unwarranted exploitation of our extrinsic substantive knowledge in employing familiar empirical models has a counterpart for analytic models. In the case of analytic models, the danger stems from an unwarranted transfer of certain formal characteristics of the model's statements to any corresponding statements in the theory of concern. In particular, the a priori characteristics (for which the terms 'analyticity' or 'logical necessity' are generally used) of statements of an analytic model are not routinely transferable to their corresponding statements in the theory of concern. While the temptation to make this kind of transfer to *observation* statements (those referring to observable features of the world) of the theory may be slight, the temptation to make the transfer to *theoretical* statements of the theory must be, perhaps, more vigilantly guarded against. Whatever the justification of the presence of theoretical (i.e., nonobservational) statements in the theory of concern—even if they turn out in some sense to be justifiably construed as analytic statements—that justification cannot depend upon the analyticity of counterpart statements in the model.[10]

7. Definitional schemata and analytical conceptual schemata

In sections 4-6 of this chapter we dealt with fully articulated scientific theories—that is, scientific theories construed as fully formalized and interpreted axiomatic systems. Now, the social scientist may aim at fully articulated theories, but much of his important scientific achievement will fall short of this for two quite distinct reasons: first, because, though the scientist may be directly aiming at the complete formulation of a theory, achieving this is simply too difficult; and second, because the scientist may not be aiming at the formulation of a theory at all, but rather at some other kind of formulation. Many present-day social-scientific formulations are, in fact, of this second, other than theoretic, kind. Thus, when an anthropologist constructs a classificational system for use in classifying societies on the basis of their kinship practices, he is doing "theoretical" work; but his formulations, though in some broad sense theoretical, are not formulations of theory—nor most importantly, are they even aimed at becoming theories. We shall use the adjective 'theoretic' to apply just to formulations that *are* designed to achieve the status of scientific theories, and reserve 'nontheoretic' to apply to other kinds of formulations which (like classificational schemata) the social scientist may also legitimately and importantly devise. In this section and the next, our attention will be focused on the problem of making some sense out of the welter of nontheoretic formulations that abound in the literature of social science.

A striking feature of the literature of social science is that it is copiously salted with nontheoretic formulations. They occur under a dizzying variety of names: 'typology,' 'typological schema,' 'conceptual schema,' 'conceptual model,' 'classificational system,' 'definitional system,' and many others. This variety seems to have proliferated wondrously, but in the almost complete absence of any uniformity of usage. Nonetheless, the formulations so bewilderingly named are, as we shall see, of only a relatively limited number of structural types. Indeed, the two types we shall examine in this section may, in a perfectly straightforward sense, be considered to be exhaustive.

In examining closely these formulations of social scientists, we can see that a significant feature of them is whether they are *constituted of statements* at all. Some are, and some are not. What we have been calling 'nontheoretic formulations' may thus be divided into those systems of formulations that contain *no* true or false sentences whatever (even when fully interpreted) and those that contain at least one sentence having a truth-value. Systems comprising the former type of formulation we shall call *definitional schemata*, or synonymously, *definitional systems*. Systems of the latter type will be referred to as *analytical conceptual schemata*, or for short, *analytical schemata*.

[10] For a discussion of this point see Braithwaite, *op. cit.*, pp. 100-111.

The difference between definitional schemata and empirical theories needs no further elaboration here than to remark that definitional schemata contain no statements (sentences that are true or false) at all. The difference between analytical schemata and empirical theories is that analytical schemata contain no empirical assertions; whatever truths they do contain are logical or analytic.[11]

a) *Definitional schemata.* This type of system of definitions consists of two sets of linguistic entities: a set W of predicates, and a set R of definitions which refer to those predicates. W will be exhaustively divisible into primitive predicates and defined predicates. R will be related to W (and indeed will *systematize* W by determining which members of W are primitive and which are not) in the following ways:

1. Every predicate in W that is referred to by an expression comprising a *definiendum* in any element (i.e., in any definition) of R, is a defined predicate of the system.
2. Every predicate in W that is referred to only in *definientia* of R, or does not occur in any element of R at all, is a primitive of the system.

Even a severely truncated example will suffice to illustrate the general characterization just given. Thus, suppose that our set W contains the usual terms of logic ('not,' 'or,' 'and,' if . . . then . . . ,' 'all,' forms of 'to be' as the copula of predication, 'some,' the sign '=' for identity, etc.), and in addition, such predicates as 'social parent,' 'social male,' 'social father,' 'social mother,' 'social brother,' 'social sister,' 'social sibling,' as well as the variables 'x,' 'y,' 'z,' 'x_1' . . . 'x_n,' which take social persons as values. Then, somewhat as follows, a set of definitions R might systemize W by establishing which of the concepts of W were generateable from any given primitive basis in W.[12]

R1. 'x is a social child of y' $=_{df}$ 'y is a social parent of x.'
R2. 'x is a social female' $=_{df}$ 'it is not the case that x is a social male.'
R3. 'x_1 is a social sibling of x' $=_{df}$ 'x_1 is a social child of some y, and that same y is male, and x_1 is a social child of some z, and that same z is a social female, and some x is a social child of that same y, and x is a social child of that same z, and it is not the case that $x_1 = x$.'
R4. 'x is a social brother' $=_{df}$ 'x is a social male and x is a social sibling of some y.'

[11] Nor are analytical schemata to be confused with analytic models of theories. Analytical schemata in science are couched in the vocabulary of the theory of concern; analytic models are, of course, couched in the vocabulary of some other theory.

[12] The example given ignores the logical terms of W, which are definitionally systematizable in routine and well-known ways not germane to our present purposes. If our purpose here were to provide a theory of definition, our characterization of R would have to be extended likewise in known ways to guarantee consistency as well as unique eliminability of defined terms by primitives.

R5. 'x is a social sister' $=_{df}$ 'x is a social female and x is a social sibling of some y.'

R6. 'x is a social father' $=_{df}$ 'x is a social male and x is a social parent of some y.'

R7. 'x is a social mother' $=_{df}$ 'x is a social female and x is a social parent of some y.'

Despite its simplicity there are several lessons to be learned from this definitional system. In the first place, its *general* adequacy for, say, anthropology, could not be determined merely from an examination of the system, for this would depend on whether the concepts that comprise the system occur in fruitful anthropological theory. Anthropologists would likely reject the example definitional system as inadequate on the grounds that the theories of kinship structure that they have (or will construct) would incorporate kinship concepts different from (e.g., wider in extension than) these. Thus, they are likely to opt for a definition of 'social sibling' that has the consequence that any two individuals who have at least *one* social parent in common are social siblings.

In the second place, even though we cannot, in the absence of appropriate theory, judge a definitional system by such a criterion of general adequacy, there are other criteria available for assessing preferability of this definitional system over alternatives. Two of these criteria are (*a*) the degree to which the definitional rules systematize the concepts, or what comes to the same thing, the degree of *structural simplicity of the system's primitive basis*, and (*b*) the *power* of the system.

The first of these criteria, systematicity or simplicity of primitive basis, has probably been an important criterion of the acceptability of theories throughout the history of science (however dimly realized the appropriate notion of simplicity may actually have been in earlier periods). We shall, in any case, be dealing further with both the criterion of simplicity and that of power. The point to be noted now, however, is that there are now means for assessing the acceptability or usefulness of scientific formulations other than theories—means that may guide both selection and construction of such nontheoretic formulations.

In the third place, though we have not included the semantical rules of designation or any other device for explicating or indicating the meanings of primitives in our general characterization of definitional schemata, it should be evident that the acceptability of such a system in empirical science will also depend in large measure upon whether the primitives have been sufficiently clarified. In the definitional system given above, if the two descriptive *primitive* predicates 'social parent' and 'social male' are wholly opaque in meaning, then so too will be the meanings of the terms defined by them in the system. If we have no idea of the meanings of the system's primitives, the system will fail altogether to have application in empirical science. Obscurity of the primitive basis *is* a ground for rejection of definitional schemata. But "sufficient clarity" is an extraordinarily difficult notion to come to grips with and, no doubt, the standards one adopts for determining it are to be sought in more basic philosophical disciplines than philosophy of social science.

Analytical conceptual schemata are closely related to definitional schemata, and some of the same criteria mentioned above as relevant to the assessment of the latter types of system are also relevant to the former types. Since relatively new and promising results have been achieved [13] in clarifying the criterion of the degree of structural simplicity or systematicity of both kinds of system, we shall say something more about this criterion, as applicable to systems, when we have completed exposition of the nature of analytical conceptual schemata in section 8.

b) Analytical conceptual schemata. This type of schema or system contains a definitional system as a subpart or component. What it includes over and above its system of definitions is a set of analytic, or logically true or "truistic," sentences. These are truistic in the sense that their truth is established not by reference to any extralinguistic empirical evidence, but rather, just by recourse to the system's definitions. Each statement in an analytical conceptual system is truistic either on the direct basis of some definitions of the system or else is a logical consequence of some set of such truistic statements (any logical consequence of a set of analytic statements is analytic).

Accordingly, we may construct an analytical conceptual schema by taking the definitional system of the social-kinship example and adding to it an appropriate set of sentences, perhaps ones like the following.

A_1 'All social brothers have at least one social parent in common.'

A_2. 'Every social individual is either a social male or a social female but not both.'

A_3. 'No social female is a social father.'

A_4. 'If anyone is a social brother then he is not a social mother.'

The truistic sentences of useful analytical schemata need not, of course, be as banal as the ones illustrated; but however complex and unobvious they do turn out to be, they will nevertheless share the characteristic feature of A_1-A_4: being able to be validated solely by recourse to the definitions of the system and logic, and not, as are empirical hypotheses, by recourse to any extralinguistic (empirical) investigations of evidence.

Both definitional schemata and analytical conceptual schemata, though themselves nontheoretic constructions in social science, are, nevertheless, presumably destined for ultimate inclusion within some social-science theory. With respect to the context of validation or justi-

---

[13] Principally by Nelson Goodman. For a brief general discussion of the topic and a list of references to published work by Goodman and others in this area, see in bibliography the reference to my article "An Introduction to Simplicity."

fication in science, their function within theories will be to assist deductive elaboration—and hence to assist in effecting the confirmation or disconfirmation of the theories of which they come to form a part. Similarly, their inclusion in theories assists the predictive and explanatory uses of such theories.

At relatively early stages of theorizing, in advance of the formulation of significantly developed theory, nontheoretic constructions, existing autonomously, also appear to play an important, but entirely heuristic, role—one which belongs, broadly speaking, to the context of discovery. In this context their significant use is that of suggesting hypotheses for test and for inclusion in theories.

8. Classificational schemata and typologies   Two types of nontheoretic formulation in social science are often referred to as *classificational schemata*. Indeed, such systems are so frequently alluded to or employed that it will be useful to see just what kinds of system they are and how they fit into the view we have been presenting. The two types of classificational schemata are (1) those in which a condition that is both necessary and sufficient for the applicability of each of the classifying terms is given, and (2) those for which such conditions are given for none, or only few, of the classificational terms. In cases of the former, the provision of a classificational schema is tantamount to the provision of a definitional schema; and however the classificational system may be represented, those of this type may be approximately equated with, or reformulated as, definitional systems. Since we have already discussed definitional systems in general, this type of classificational system will detain us only briefly.[14]

The second type of classificational schema, the type most often so dubbed, is more appropriately construed as a species of *analytical schema*. Its special characteristics deserve separate discussion. In general, we shall treat a classificational schema as that kind of nontheoretic system which lays down conditions for the applicability of its categorial (classificatory) terms.[15]

Every classificational schema will presuppose explicitly or implicitly its *universe of discourse*—the range of entities to which the terms

[14] While some classificational schemata are thus appropriately construed as definitional, the converse is not true: not all definitional schemata are classificational. The example system of section 7 is not a classificational system. In the extant social-science literature, systems that are in fact definitional are still only rarely represented in the standard definitional notation of logic illustrated in section 7. Such systems are usually quite loosely presented, either wholly discursively or in only a partially formalized manner; and where they are explicitly dubbed *classificational schemata*, they are also sometimes presented diagrammatically.

[15] One might regard (and doubtless this is the preponderant practice in the social and biological sciences) a classificational schema as "dividing up" its extralinguistic universe of discourse (i.e., "dividing up" what the terms refer to) rather than as providing conditions for the applicability of terms. Here we make the "linguistic turn" and choose the latter mode of speaking, in line with the consideration advanced in c of section 3.

comprising the schema apply. In the first type of classificational schema—
the type we assimilated to a definitional system—the categorial terms
may be such that each entity of the universe of discourse will be designated by (or in the denotation of) one, and no more than one, categorial term.[16] Thus, if we specify social individuals as our universe of
discourse, and indicate that 'female' is definitionally equivalent to 'not
male,' then the categorial terms 'male' and 'female' will be mutually
exclusive and exhaustive of that universe of discourse, i.e., each entity
in the universe of discourse will have exactly one of the categorial terms
'male' or 'female' applicable to it.

Of course, most classificational schemata are more ramified than
this illustration of dichotomous categorials. Ramification may be achieved
in two ways: through employment of a set of more than two categorial
terms (which may still be mutually exclusive and together exhaustive
of some specified universe of discourse), and also by an accretion of
universes of discourse hierarchically related.

The first kind of ramification would be illustrated by alternating
the way of defining 'female' from that given above, and by adding, say,
'eunuch,' defined as 'neither male nor female,' as a third categorial term.
There is no limit to the number of terms that may be in such a set,
while together, the members of the set remain, *logically*, exhaustive and
mutually exclusive relative to their universe of discourse.

The second kind of ramification is, so to speak, longitudinal rather
than latitudinal, and is, perhaps, best thought of as adding levels or
making the classificational schema hierarchical. One would add to the
dichotomous example first given above, an indication that, say, the *subordinate* universe of discourse designated by 'male' is itself exhausted by
the mutually exclusive subcategorials 'married male' and 'unmarried
male.'

Again, each entity of the subordinate universe of discourse will
be designated by exactly one of the subcategorials. Note that in hierarchically ramified schemata every entity to which a subcategorial applies
will also be designated by the corresponding categorial—and in general,
in an extended hierarchy, by every corresponding supercategorial in the
hierarchical chain, should there be more than two levels (i.e., if there
are *sub*-subordinate universes of discourse) specified.

What has just been outlined applies to those classificational
schemata assimilable to definitional systems that partition or divide all
their universes of discourse exclusively and exhaustively and by virtue
of logical means alone. On the other hand, classificational schemata
that are not thus assimilable, those we have been construing as species
of analytical schemata, will either fail to partition some of their respective universes of discourse exclusively or exhaustively, or else, if they do
partition all of them exclusively and exhaustively, it will not be by
virtue of logical means alone, but because of some contingent feature of

---

[16] Or by the definitional equivalent of such a term.

the world (e.g., the contingent absence of any entities to which a "missing" categorial *would* apply).

Such classificational analytical schemata, like classificational definitional systems, may have great heuristic value (and not least, on those occasions when they reveal contingently empty categories) in suggesting empirical hypotheses and theories. Again, though they may come to be incorporated as constituents of empirical theories, it is, nevertheless, important to remember that these classificational analytical schemata are nontheoretic systems—not, in themselves, containing statements that are susceptible to empirical test. In sum, neither of the two kinds of classificational schemata can be subjected to empirical test in the sense in which full theoretical systems (theories or models) may. This is why we refer to such classificational schemata as *nontheoretic* formulations.

The popularity of *nontheoretic* formulations in social-science literature is great, and if the relative frequency of their employment is any indication of their usefulness, they are very useful indeed.

Some notion of why and how theorists of social science use them may be gained by considering a quotation from the work of an influential writer in the field of sociology: Talcott Parsons. The quotation does not follow the precise formal usage of some of the terms we have more rigorously introduced in earlier sections; we use it here for illustrative purposes because in it Parsons seems clearly and explicitly to be recognizing that the propositions of a classificational analytical schema do not "admit of . . . empirical proof." The specific character or substantive burden of Parson's "Theory of Action" is not germane to our present concerns. (It will suffice, perhaps, to point out by way of background that Parsons uses the term 'pattern variables' to refer to what is encompassed in a classificational system whose universe of discourse is the kinds of choices that can be made by a social or psychological actor in a social or psychological situation.)

In characterizing his own "theory" in this relatively recent statement, Parsons tells us: [17]

> Both the pattern variables and the four system-problems are conceptual schemes, or sets of categories, for classifying the components of action. They provide a frame of reference within which such classification can be made. The figures presented below indicate the methods, sets of

[17] One should not conclude from this quotation that Parsons' "Theory of Action" is a nontheoretical formulation—despite his apparent endorsement of such a conclusion, there is independent evidence that Parsons is simply wrong here about the nature of his own work. In fact, frequently (e.g., see the paragraph immediately following the one quoted) in "Pattern Variables Revisited" (see bibliography), he says things that are incompatible with the quoted view. Of course, the fact that Parsons may be wrong about his own "theory" (as is likely in the quotation employed) does not make that quotation any less apt an illustration for our present purposes. The quotation does show how some sociological theorists view the character of what they take to be classificational analytical schemata.

rules and procedures, that state how these categories may be used analytically; they imply *theorems*—propositions that admit of logical, not empirical proof—which state a set of determinate relationships among the categories and, in so doing, outline a *theory* of action.[18]

As we might expect from our own knowledge of the nature of classificational analytical schemata, some of the propositions with which Parsons furnishes us, and which are presumably analytic or logically true (i.e., they are presumably propositions admitting 'of logical, not empirical proof'), are ones that apparently provide a necessary, or a sufficient, condition for the application of some of his pattern-variable (categorial) terms.

Typologies. We turn now to still another social-science term, 'typology,' used in connection with systematic formulations of various kinds. Of all the terms descriptive of formulations in the social sciences, 'typology' is perhaps the most frequently used. It has been employed to refer not only to the various kinds of nontheoretic formulation already described, but also to a great many others, ranging from vague formulations containing so-called "polar" concepts (whose meaning or application may have been indicated in only the most casual fashion) through more elaborate formulations of groups of concepts systematically connected by a few accompanying analytic sentences, and finally, to quite sophisticated systems of comparative ordering or measurement. These last mentioned systems may occasionally achieve the status of theoretic formulations by incorporating empirically testable statements.

In terms of the foregoing considerations, the great bulk of formulations referred to as typologies will, in fact, turn out to be definitional systems or analytical conceptual systems of varying degrees of power and systematism (or simplicity) formulated with varying degrees of explicitness. Those typologies that purport to *order* the entities in their universe of discourse or range of application, however, have not yet received our attention.

Although it is not within the province of this book to embark on a full exposition of the complex topic of systems that impose an ordering upon, or make possible the measurement of, the things in the universe of discourse to which they apply, some elementary and introductory comments about such systems may help to place them in clearer perspective.

Consider a universe of discourse of individual entities determined by some concept or other (e.g., *sticks* or *stones* or *cabbages* or *kings* or *national economies* or *human beings*). Let us refer to any set of things comprised in such a universe of discourse, or domain, as the set *D*. Now,

---

[18] *Ibid.*, pp. 467-68. Incidentally, the authoritativeness of this article as a current "last word" by Parsons on just what does constitute his general "Theory of Action" is borne out by his essay "The Point of View of the Author," p. 335 *n* (see bibliography), where he refers the reader to the very article from which we quoted above for an "account of the pattern variables and the way in which they fit into the general action scheme. . . ."

if our typology contains a classificatory or a categorial concept M, applicable to some but not all the members of D, then, by employing M (using the criterion for its application that is presumably furnished by knowing its meaning) we may divide D into two subsets: one containing each member of D that M is *true of*, or applies to, and one containing each member of D that M is not true of. Now, suppose instead of a property-term like M (e.g., 'male') we employed a dyadic relation-term R (e.g., 'father of'). Assuming that R has some exemplifications in D, it too would divide D into two subsets. However, since R applies not to single individuals, but to pairs of individuals, one of these subsets would be a subset, each member of which was a certain kind of pair of individuals of D (e.g., a father-and-child pair); the other subset would not contain any pairs to which R was applicable.

Among all of the relations applicable to pairs of elements of D, we can distinguish two possibilities: those which are *serial-ordering* relations relative to D, and those which are not. To claim that any R is serially ordering relative to D, or that it establishes a serial ordering among all the elements of D, has the import that certain statements about that relation R are true. In particular, it is to claim that, with respect to D, R is a transitive, irreflexive, asymmetrical, and connected relation.[19]

Reverting explicitly to the topic of typological systems, two points may now be emphasized. First, a typology may consist both of concepts that distinguish certain (e.g., polar) positions in a domain D ordered by some ordering relation R, and also of that concept R as well. Thus, if D is constituted of a class of unequally aged U.S. citizens our typology might consist of the polar concepts 'elderly citizen' and 'juvenile citizen' and also the ordering relation or concept 'older than.'

Secondly, a typological system may be construed as also including the *statements* making the claims that are sufficient to guarantee an ordering of D by R.

If the relation-term is itself explicated in such a way that the included assertions determining that relation's transitivity, irreflexivity, asymmetry, and connectedness are themselves analytic or logically true

---

[19] R is *irreflexive* relative to D if none of the things in D stands in the relation R to itself. R is *asymmetrical* relative to D if for every pair of things x and y in D of which it is true to claim that x stands in the relation R to y, it is *false* to claim that y stands in R to x. R is *transitive* relative to D if for any three different entities x, y, and z of D, it is true to say 'If x has R to y and y has R to z, then x has R to z.' 'Taller than' is an example of a relation that, for a D consisting of physical objects, would be *irreflexive* (no physical object is taller than itself), *asymmetric* (if a first physical object is taller than a second, it is false that the second is taller than the first), and *transitive* (if x is taller than y and y taller than z, then x is taller than z). Finally, R is *connected* relative to D if for any pair of members x and y of D, either x has R to y or else y has R to x. Thus, if D consists of a class of *unequally aged* citizens of the U. S., and if our relation-term R is the term 'older than,' then of every two members x and y in the class mentioned, it will be true either that x is older than y or else that y is older than x.

statements, then the typological system will in fact be just the kind of system we distinguished earlier as an analytical conceptual schema. On the other hand, if any of these assertions is a *contingent* or *empirical*, rather than analytic, statement, the entire theoretical formulation becomes a theory or a theoretic portion of a theory. (It is, in this case, not a nontheoretic formulation of any sort.)

So far we have touched upon only those order-establishing typologies whose ordering relation *serially* orders the things in the typology's universe of discourse. More frequently encountered in the social sciences among order-establishing typologies are those which contain a *pair* of relations that *together* establish a *quasi-serial* ordering of D.

The notion of quasi-serial ordering is intuitively rather obvious. For example, if the D of our typology consists not of a restricted class of unequally aged U.S. citizens, but of the wider class of *all* U.S. citizens, then the relation 'older than' will fail to establish a serial ordering among the members of this class. In particular, the connectivity requirement will not have been met, since for some pairs of U.S. citizens—just those pairs of individuals who are of the *same age*—the relation 'older than' will not hold. If, however, our typology also incorporates an appropriate second relation, and if this second relation has the characteristics of being transitive, reflexive, and symmetrical relative to D, then the two relations together may establish a *quasi-serial* ordering among the members of this wider universe of discourse. The kind of second relation required is called an *equivalence relation*, and in this case, the appropriate equivalence relation would be 'is the same age as.'

In general, a universe of discourse D that is not serially orderable by some relation R, may still be *quasi-serially* orderable by the pair of relations R and E when the following three complex conditions hold: R is transitive, irreflexive, and asymmetrical; E is transitive, reflexive, and symmetrical; and for every pair of elements of D for which R does *not* hold, E does hold, and conversely, for every pair for which E does not hold R does hold.

In sum, the kind of typological system we have been discussing (i.e., typological systems not appropriately construable *simply* as classificational systems) will contain at least the following.

1. a concept determining the typology's universe of discourse
2. some relation(s) that determine(s) an ordering (e.g., a serial or a quasi-serial ordering) among the members of the universe of discourse
3. statements implying that certain features (e.g., transitivity) characterize the relation(s) (if these statements are analytic the typology is a *nontheoretic* formulation; if any are contingent, the typology is theoretic)
4. a set of concepts (frequently a "polar-pair" or "extreme-opposites") usually designating some specific members of the universe of discourse that are "distant" from each other or at opposite ends of

the array into which the ordering relation(s) *order* the members
of the universe of discourse [20]

Upon examining many of the typologies that have received great
attention in the various social sciences, we see that their frequent defectiveness as usable components of social-science theory stems from failure
to fulfill the requirements of items 2 and 3 above. Typologies containing concepts such as *'Gemeinschaft'* and *'Gesellschaft,'* 'perfect competition' and 'monopoly,' 'introvert' and 'extrovert,' 'urban' and 'rural,'
'folkways' and 'mores,' 'open society' and 'closed society,' 'inner directed'
and 'other directed' furnish examples that are easily come by. They have
been presented and ruminated over with enough *obiter dicta* to make it
perfectly clear that not only the authors and advocates of these systems,
but their critics as well, construe the respective typological systems as
having ordered universes of discourse. Some personalities are *more intro-
verted than* others; some markets or economies are *closer to being perfectly competitive than* others; some societies are *more open than* others,
etc. This sort of implicit or explicit ordering *is* unmistakably the import
of such typologies as usually presented or discussed.

The ordering of the universes of discourse for scientific theorizing is
thus highly desirable, yet almost all typologies that occur in the literature
have failed, as have those just cited, to provide the explicit theoretical
framework that such systems of ordering require for rigor. Why?

Well, not primarily because of the defectiveness of the concepts
that *are* made relatively explicit in such typologies—the concepts determining the universe of discourse and the so-called type-concepts designating distinguished members of the universe of discourse. To be sure,
such concepts are often presented with annoying vagueness or looseness.
But this vagueness is, in general, remediable in relatively easy ways; and
one way or another, such remedies for vagueness of reference have come
to be suggested in the literature. The crucial difficulties hindering the
usefulness of such schemata stem rather from an ignorance of the need
for *explicating* the ordering-relation concepts that must form a necessary
constituent of the schemata, or else from the recalcitrance of such relation concepts to actual attempts at explication.

We are, for example, likely to agree that an "open" society (or a
"wholly" or "perfectly" open society) is one in which no form of

---

[20] So-called "rank-orderings" or "systems of ranking" in the literature of social
science will usually be found to be like the typologies described above except for a
characteristic *notational* difference: instead of choosing names or descriptive terms
like 'introvert,' 'monopoly,' 'intuitive,' 'secular society,' *'Gemeinschaft* grouping,' etc.,
to designate members (or "positions") in the ordered universe of discourse, advantage
is taken of the familiar *ordinal* characteristics associated with numerals or letters of
the alphabet. These latter systematic numeral or letter notations are applied in such
a fashion as to fulfill both the function of designating members (hence, substituting
for nominational words) and simultaneously (by virtue of our independent familiarity with their indigenous ordinal characteristics), indicating that member's "position" relative to other thus designated members.

governmental censorship on media of communication is countenanced. But if two societies x and y are alike except for the fact that x censors only movies while y censors only comic books, is x more open than y? We cannot even begin to answer such a question until we are given a much more rigorous explication of the appropriate ordering relation(s) than has been given heretofore by theorizers. And of course such theories are defective at least to the extent that we are not provided with such explications. Whatever import such vague typologies do have must be merely suggestive or heuristic (and the absence of any viable "suggested" theory imposes pessimism even here). That import surely fails to be theoretic.

We have, so far, discussed only the character of typologies that order their universes of discourse serially or quasi-serially. Such orderings may not be quantitative—in the sense that they may not allow us to say such simple things as, the length of x added to the length of y equals the length of z. A much more powerful kind of typological system than the *serial* ones thus far considered would be one that imposed a *metrical* ordering upon its universe of discourse, that is, a typological system that would enable us to make *quantitative measurements*.[21]

The formidable problems associated with the development of typologies able to determine a metrical ordering, preclude a full and rigorous treatment in any context that (like the present one) claims to limit itself to an introduction to problems of social science. Nevertheless, the discussion already undertaken in this and preceding sections may enable us again to provide briefly an inkling of what is involved in these more complex systems.

The ordering-relation concepts of a metrically ordered typology must fulfill a stronger set of conditions than the relations of serially-ordering, or quasi-serially-ordering typology—stronger in the precise sense that the *metrical* relations R_m and E_m, fulfill all of the serial conditions (or quasi-serial conditions) of R and E, and some further conditions as well.

Now, it will be remembered that serially-ordering typological systems have as constituents some set of statements determining requisite characteristics (e.g., transitivity) of the ordering relations involved. For metrical typologies this set of determining statements must be augmented. Indeed, for metricization to be fully achieved these statements of the typological system *must be such that the axiom set of some number theory* (e.g., the theory of rational numbers, or the theory of real numbers, or the theory of complex numbers) actually constitutes a *model* of these statements. If, and only if, such a model relationship does hold, do the requisite theorems (e.g., of additivity) from the model number theory have corresponding *translations in* the typological system—trans-

---

[21] See bibliography for Churchman's and Hempel's (*Fundamentals of Concept Formation in Empirical Science*) illuminating discussions of the logic of systems of measurement, of their desirability in science, and of the formidable problems associated with their construction.

lations which, in turn, actually establish the metrical ordering (i.e., the quantitative measurability) of the members of the system's universe of discourse. And, of course, the power of such a metrical typology is precisely that conferred on theories with mathematical models, as noted in section 6.

The construction of metrical typologies has thus far been achieved only rarely in social science. For the most part, such achievements have been confined to subdisciplines within economics or psychology.

There is *no* evidence whatever to support the view that the reason for the rarity with which metricization has been achieved in social science is due to an innate or intrinsic nonmeasurability of phenomena with which social scientists are concerned—though these are reasons which have been alleged for the rarity. Further consideration of the alleged greater complexity of social science will be discussed in section 13.

9. Systematization and simplicity   In this, and in section 7, our attention has been focused upon various kinds of nontheoretic formulations that occur in social science; in other words, we have been concerned with kinds of systematic constructions that are *different* from empirical theories. Now, empirical theories are assessed for their acceptability on the basis of being confirmed or disconfirmed by experimental and other tests. But this sort of assessment is precisely what is logically unavailable for nontheoretic formulations. By their very nature, nontheoretic formulations (since they are neither single hypotheses nor sets of systematically related hypotheses) are not susceptible to confirmation or disconfirmation. But if they cannot be confirmed or disconfirmed, by what criteria *can* nontheoretic formulations be assessed or validated or justified?

In any scientific discipline rich in theory this problem might be considered less serious. Since nontheoretic formulations are designed for inclusion as constituents of theories, in such disciplines the likelihood is high that we would encounter nontheoretic formulations primarily as already incorporated in theories. Accordingly, we could sensibly choose to assess these formulations in conformity with our assessment of the very theories of which they become a part in such sciences.

But the social sciences are poor in theory.[22] In fact, it would probably be fair to say that a vast preponderance of all the formulations constituting the output of social scientists consists of just such nontheoretic formulations as we have discussed above. Thus, it makes considerably less sense—at least at the present state of social science—to rest our ability to assess nontheoretic formulations upon the validation of theories (that do not even exist but) that might come to incorporate them. For this reason it becomes urgent to consider whether there are

---

[22] Why they are is, itself, an important and intriguing problem of both the philosophy of science and the sociology of science toward the solution of which, however, very little progress has been made.

any criteria for directly assessing in social science nontheoretic formulations themselves.

When the question of criteria for directly assessing the acceptability of nontheoretic formulations was broached earlier in this chapter, four criteria were mentioned: the *theoretic fruitfulness* of such systems' concepts, and also the *clarity, power,* and *simplicity* of their primitive bases—i.e., their sets of primitive terms.

We need not linger over the first two criteria. Theoretic fruitfulness of a nontheoretic system is determined, in the context of validation, by the number and centrality of the laws in which its concepts occur. In the absence, already noted, of much theory in social science, we must reconcile ourselves to doing little with this criterion for the present. Clarity of primitive basis, as was indicated earlier in this chapter, is not only a problematic criterion, but the problems it poses belong to the more generic philosophical disciplines, philosophy of science and epistemology, rather than to philosophy of social science.[23] Power and simplicity, are, however, appropriate concerns for us.

The *power* of the primitive basis of a nontheoretic system, say, the definitional system S_D, may be equated with that system's range or scope of application. Since all of the defined terms of S_D are defined by its primitives, it should be clear that their range of application, the entities to which they apply, or (adopting a usage standard in semantics) their *extensions,* must already be included within the extensions of the primitives. Consequently, in assessing the power of S_D, what we are assessing is the power of S_D's primitive basis.

There are, despite recent significant advances, still a great many problems to be solved before an adequate general means for measuring the power of any system will be available. (See bibliography for works by Kemeny and Svenonius, and in particular, see Goodman's "The Test of Simplicity" and "Recent Developments in the Theory of Simplicity," for rigorous technical discussions of these advances and problems.) Nevertheless, even some very elementary considerations concerning the comparison of systems with respect to power will help indicate what is at stake.

If, for example, the sum of the extensions of the primitives of a definitional system S_D is a proper part of (i.e., is wholly contained within but does not exhaust) the sum of the extensions of the primitives of S_D', then S_D' has a wider range or scope, or greater power, than S_D. Such a discrimination will be useful to us when notions of the range of phenomena to which the predicates of the two definitional systems being compared apply, are clear enough to enable us to tell whether a system in question has too narrow or too broad a scope to be usable within some theory. But discriminations concerning power will also be

[23] For a profound discussion of *clarity* and other criteria for selection of primitive bases, see Nelson Goodman's *The Structure of Appearance.* This important book also furnishes the best discussion of the theory of formulations of systems that has been presented in recent years.

useful when—as is doubtless the case in the social sciences—our antecedent knowledge is at a considerably less advanced state too. For instance, though we are not by any means certain what all the things that should cogently be called "social actions" are, nevertheless, we are sure enough about some of the things that should be so called. Accordingly, the knowledge that S_D' has at least these latter things in its scope while S_D does not, will furnish us with some basis for the decision that S_D' is a more adequate system for inclusion in a *theory* of social action than is S_D.

But all of the above are preliminary and rather obvious considerations on the problem of how to characterize or assess nontheoretic systems. A much less obvious criterion than power, but perhaps much more important one at the present stage of the social sciences, is the economy or structural simplicity of or degree of systematization accomplished by, a system. Two systems may be equal in power without at all being equal in economy. Just as one economy of an automobile is estimated not by the distance it travels, but by how much gasoline it requires to go that distance, so also with the economy of systems. The power of a system is analogous to the distance traveled by our automobile in that merely knowing it will not measure its economy. In like fashion, to arrive at the economy of a system we require some independent measure of the simplicity of its basis—i.e., of its primitive predicates.

Now, allusions to simplicity in present-day science and in the historical literature of the sciences and of philosophy are immensely varied in intent and nuance. Before any very fruitful consideration of the topic can be undertaken it is necessary to delimit to some extent the range of our attention. This can be accomplished by fitting, with a minimum of Procrustean ferocity, all of the immensely varied references to simplicity under a relatively uncomplicated classificational schema.[24]

Uses of 'simplicity,' then, may be classified either as *ontological* (i.e., extralinguistic) or *descriptional* (i.e., linguistic). Subclassifications under both these main rubrics are *subjective* (i.e., psychological) and *objective* (i.e., nonpsychological). Moreover, under *descriptional* it is useful as well to distinguish *notational* and *logical* (or *structural*) as subclassifications of the kinds of simplicity. A few examples will provide the very rough degree of clarity that is all we require at the outset for these six categorial terms.

Consider, first, ontological simplicity. It is quite clear that many people have used the term 'simplicity' or its cognates to attribute certain characteristics to the universe rather than to our descriptions of the universe. For such individuals it has been the extralinguistic universe, or some segment of it, that is said to exhibit or to fail to exhibit

[24] The one we are about to employ is suggested, though not precisely in this form, in Chap. 1 of Ackermann's searching thesis and is employed by myself in "An Introduction to Simplicity." (See bibliography for both listings.)

some degree or other of simplicity. Further, these attributions of ontological simplicity may be classed as either objective or subjective, depending upon whether their import is that the universe is (or is not) simple independently of how we perceive it or whether the (extra-linguistic) universe is (or is not) perceived by us as simple. If 'simplicity' is used to apply to the universe independently of the perception of it, we shall classify that usage as objective-ontological, if 'simplicity' is taken as a predicate of our (extralinguistic) responses to the (extralinguistic) universe, we shall classify it as *subjective-ontological*.

Attributions of simplicity both to the universe and to our extra-linguistic responses to it, abound in the literature of science and metaphysics. Such attributions are often obscure and problematic. But these are not the subject of our present interest. Indeed, having reminded ourselves of their occurrence, we need only note that it is not ontological simplicity but descriptional simplicity that we wish to clarify.

Turning, then, to linguistic considerations, we may distinguish under the general category of descriptional simplicity and its two subcategories, objective and subjective simplicity to sub-subcategories: notational and logical simplicity.[25] An attribution of simplicity to a description on the basis of a notational property of it, such as the number of inscriptions (e.g., of letters) it contains, independently of anyone's psychological response to such a property, will be classed as an instance of *objective-notational simplicity*. On the other hand, an attribution of simplicity to a description on the basis of the familiarity of the notation, the elegance of the notation, its convenience, its efficiency for manipulation, or because of any aesthetic quality it has, etc., may count as instances of *subjective-notational simplicity*.

But neither objective- nor subjective-notational simplicity is our ultimate topic of concern. What we shall be concerned with is the *logical* (or, synonymously, the *structural*) simplicity of formations. Moreover, since our interest is not in how people psychologically respond to logical properties of theories, we may characterize our field of attention as *objective-logical simplicity*. Hereafter, all references to simplicity, unless otherwise qualified, are intended as references to objective-logical simplicity.

Realization of the importance of considerations of simplicity for inductive problems in the philosophy of science is a phenomenon of the relatively recent past. This is not altogether surprising in view of the fact that most of the advances in logic, upon application of which much

[25] Whether, in fact, any radical distinction between the *notational* and *logical* simplicity of descriptions is an ultimately tenable one is, itself, still debatable. However, this is not a point at issue in the present context. In employing the distinction we mean merely to call attention to such differing characteristics of formulations as, say, their brevity in contrast with the logical *degrees* of the predicates they contain, i.e., such logical characteristics as the predicates' being property-terms (first degree); dyadic relation-terms (second degree); triadic relation-terms (third degree); and so forth.

of the significant work accomplished has depended, were not made until this century. Despite the importance of achieving an adequate explication of the concept, sustained and significant work toward its accomplishment has thus far been undertaken by only a relatively small circle of philosophers. In the quite recent past interest in the problem has grown under the impetus of the positive and detailed results achieved by Goodman in particular, and we can look forward with hopeful excitement to further significant advances.

Perhaps the importance of attaining an adequate explication of simplicity can best be indicated by again pointing out some aspects of its connection with *systematization* (see bibliography for Goodman's "The Test of Simplicity," the brief opening remarks of which are as illuminating as any that have been made on the topic):

> All scientific activity amounts to the invention of and the choice among systems of hypotheses. One of the primary considerations guiding this process is that of simplicity. Nothing could be much more mistaken than the traditional idea that we first seek a true system and then, for the sake of elegance alone, seek a simple one. We are inevitably concerned with simplicity as soon as we are concerned with system at all; for system is achieved just to the extent that the basic vocabulary and set of first principles used in dealing with the given subject matter are simplified. When simplicity of basis vanishes to zero—that is, when no term or principle is derived from any of the others—system also vanishes to zero. Systematization is the same thing as simplification of basis.

In science, the connection of systematization with simplicity is of the utmost importance. System, as was indicated earlier, is no mere adornment of science; it is science's very heart. To say this is not merely to deny that it is science's business to heap up unrelated, haphazard, or disconnected bits of information, it is also to point out that it is an ideal of science to give an *organized* account of the universe. It is an ideal of science to connect, to fit together in logical relations, the concepts and statements embodying whatever knowledge has been acquired. Such organization is, in fact, a necessary condition for the accomplishment of two of science's chief functions: explanation and prediction.

The work that has been done, and the work currently being done, on objective-logical simplicity has not given us a complete and adequate explication of the concept. It has had, for its students, the opposite effect of bringing a clearer realization of precisely how its problems ramify and of how much remains to be done.

Attempts such as Goodman's, to clarify the notion of the simplicity of systems, might be thought to have an obvious focus on the simplicity of sets of axioms or postulates. Thus, a first impulse in characterizing the simplicity of systems might be to say that of two otherwise equally adequate formalizations, the one with fewer axioms or postulates is, objectively, simpler. However, little reflection is needed to show that this suggestion is not very helpful; on the other hand, its lack of promise leads naturally to a consideration of the simplicity of a formulation's set of primitive predicates rather than of its axioms. For the number of axioms (assuming it is finite) of any formulation can be trivially reduced to one by the simple operation of conjunction. By the criterion of number of axioms every formulation would thus be trivially equivalent to one that was maximally simple. (A *conjunction* is any set of statements connected by the logical operation usually expressed in English by the word 'and.') Nor would it be possible to ameliorate this unwelcome result by any stipulation regarding the number of conjuncts in a set of axioms. For, any pair of conjuncts may be trivially reduced to a corresponding unconjoined statement by appropriate definitions involving the predicates originally contained in those conjuncts. This indicates that to get at a relevant sense of 'simplicity' we must go beyond considerations of the number, or gross logical structure, of axioms when they occur in formulations; instead, we must come to grips with the logical structure of the predicates themselves in the predicate bases of scientific formulations.

Since it is not implausible to assume that the formulations of science all share a common apparatus of *logical* expressions, this means that our attention must turn to the structural simplicity of the *extralogical* expressions, the extralogical predicates, for the assessment of simplicity differences among scientific formulations. And this is, indeed, the route that has been followed in work on the problem. In the course of several years of such work, and through a process of increasingly successful modifications, Goodman has been able to construct a system of measurement that provides a means for assessing the simplicity of predicate bases of fully formalized systems. In general (and here, vaguely), Goodman's assignments of simplicity-values may be thought of as depending on the manner in which the extralogical primitive predicates of a system *organize* (by virtue of such of their logical properties as reflexivity or of symmetry) the entities comprised in the total extension of the system.

Before leaving this topic, two things must be emphasized: first, the special importance of the problem for the social sciences, and second, the limitations of our present instruments for measuring simplicity despite the advances already made.

The problem of acquiring an adequate measure of simplicity is crucially important for the logic of induction itself. Philosophers of science, and many scientists, too, have recently come to realize more clearly that an adequate logic of induction—that is, an adequate body of methodological principles or criteria on the basis of which judgments about the acceptability of scientific theories may be cogently based, will have to take into account other things than the evidence for or against such theories.[26] Such additional characteristics of theories as the structural simplicity of their bases need also to be taken into account.

Indeed, it is not unfair to say that so long as we do not have an adequate measure of the simplicity of theories, we fail also to have an adequate logic of induction. But the notion of simplicity has a special importance for social science. For any success in providing a measure of the simplicity of the predicate bases of theories would also provide us with a measure of the simplicity of nontheoretic systems— systems such as the ones we have been examining in this and section 7. And as has been noted, nontheoretic systems of various kinds, that is, just the formulations not susceptible to *evidential* test, seem to play a predominant role in social science, at least in its present stage. Accordingly, the availability of a simplicity measure would mean that we would not have to respond with either despair or indifference to, say, Parsons' assertion that his system is not empirically testable; we could still assess that system and accept or reject it on relevant systematic grounds.

Again, for example, of two *definitional* systems supposedly of equal scope, both of which were candidates for ultimate inclusion in some theory of social action, there would be measurable grounds for choosing the more simple over the less simple: all other things being equal, a theory incorporating the former would be inductively more highly validated or acceptable than a theory incorporating the latter. Specifically, the degree to which, say, a definitional system systematizes, will be what is at issue. For example, in weighing two systems against each other, what is measured by the criterion of simplicity is, in a sense, the relative narrowness of alternative primitive bases, each of the two alternatives being sufficient for the generation of the entire set of terms required to apply the system.

But, it might be said, what is the good of all this talk of measuring simplicity when a prerequisite to the application of any such measuring device as Goodman's is the *full formalization* of the system to be measured? And Parson's General "Theory" of Social Action, like most formulations in social science, is as far from full formalization as can readily be imagined. This brings us directly to the second point to be emphasized, namely, that in its present status, the system for measuring simplicity is scarcely employable in the social sciences. The attention we have been giving the concept is warranted by its potential usefulness and must not be taken as suggesting the ready availability of means for making the wanted measurements.

In fact, the problem of achieving the full formalization of social-science formulations, which is a prerequisite for the application of Goodman's results on simplicity, is a peculiarly thorny one. As was noticed earlier, only a few theories in all science achieve formalization. There is possibly no need to labor the point that with respect to the systematiza-

[26] Cf. Carl Hempel's important book *Philosophy of Natural Science*, Prentice-Hall Foundations of Philosophy Series, and my articles on value judgments, validation, and simplicity cited in the bibliography.

tion of theories of social science we shall have to rest content with something considerably short of full formalization. This raises at least two related questions. First, is there any way of telling how far we can (or ought to) go toward explicit formalization at any given stage of inquiry? Second, and perhaps equally important, can we give a relatively clear meaning to the concept of *partial formalization*—or to put the question in another and more useful way, is there some way of systematically explaining or constructing techniques of partial formalization, which could be fruitfully applied on at least those occasions that call for simplicity assessments of scientific formulations? The accomplishment of this latter task would mean that we must become self-conscious about techniques of partial formalization and that suitable modifications of Goodman's device for measuring simplicity be effected in such a way that *it* may become applicable also to partially formalized systems.

10. Partial formalization   The term 'partial formalization' will be construed to apply to both theoretic and nontheoretic formulations in social science. In discussing elementary aspects of the subject, we shall count as partial formalizations those negligibly formalized systems exhibiting even one supposedly deductive connection among its statements, or which determine *explicitly* the usage of even one constituent concept. On the other hand, we shall still count as only a partial formalization an *almost* complete elaboration of a theory as a deductive system.

This wide range at once suggests that we need some way of characterizing the *degrees* of partial formalization, or alternatively, the degree to which a system falls short of full formalization. In fact, what seems to be needed is a good deal of hard work in clarifying the notion of degree of partial formalization as well as the notion of differing *types* of partial formalization. Unfortunately, little work seems to have been done up to the present. Accordingly, the survey that follows should be regarded as the most rudimentary sort of attempt to clarify the general outlines of the problems presented rather than as attempts to present results achieved.

We might begin by asking what kind of modification would have to be made in, say, Goodman's system for measuring simplicity in order to apply that device to some partial formalization. The answer here seems straightforward. Ordinarily, what we lack in systems falling short of full formalization is definitive knowledge of which of the concepts occurring in the system are to be counted as *the primitives* of what might be a future perspicuous (or even *any*) full formalization. Thus, what we would seem to require is a method for making sound projections about the logical character of such future formulations on the basis of whatever information we *do* have. Similarly, since partially formalized theories will usually not exhibit the logical structure of the putative primitives, some method for making sound projections or otherwise handling this omission must also be found.

Both of the problems just mentioned suggest that attention to a few frequently exemplified properties of partial formalization may be rewarding. These are comprised in a technique of partial formalization that we shall refer to as *systematic presupposition.*

a) *Systematic presupposition in theories.* An often encountered concomitant of *partial* formalization, is the *implicit presupposition* of large segments of a field or discipline *other* than that to which the theory being constructed is indigenous.

Even a cursory glance at general elementary text books in such fields as physics, chemistry, biology, psychology, sociology, and anthropology will reveal that exposition in any of them employs some *nonindigenous* concepts without explication and in presupposition of the antecedent clarity of such nonindigenous concepts. Thus, in a physics text one is not likely to find explication of the concepts of logic—concepts nonindigenous to physics—like 'all,' 'not,' 'or,' etc., that are nevertheless essentially employed in the text. In chemistry, nonindigenous terms like 'mass' and 'temperature' may occur, generally unexplicated; this also holds true for the occurrence of such nonindigenous terms as 'length' and 'elastic' in biology, 'biological organism' in psychology, and 'biological evolution' or 'hunger' in sociology and anthropology. These and scores of other terms not indigenous to a theory patently presupposing them to be already understood, ordinarily are employed not as primitive *in* the theory, but in a fashion to be distinguished from those not explicitly defined terms that *are* indigenous to the theory, and that may well come to be employed as the theory's indigenous primitives.

Some of what follows will be illuminated by pursuing this distinction further. We have been saying that a partially formalized formulation may comprise two kinds of terms or concepts that are *unexplicated* or undefined in that formulation: (*a*) concepts *indigenous* to the theory and that at any given time may have the status of *relative primitives* and (*b*) concepts not indigenous to the theory and that may have a distinctive status still to be determined. We are speaking here of indigenous concepts in the sense in which, e.g., 'mass,' through long and distinguished entrenchment in physical theories would be recognized as a "term of physics" or in which 'neurosis' would be recognized as a "term of psychology." A more precise or adequate definition of 'indigenous primitive,' however, presents formidable difficulties, and any attempt to surmount these would take us beyond the scope of this book. What already has been said will suffice at least to introduce the notion.

The importance of focusing attention on nonindigenous terms in partially formalized theories rests in the fact that their occurrence will usually indicate that *some portion* (large or small) *of the results of some other discipline or area of knowledge is being presupposed* in the theory. Thus, for example, the occurrence of 'temperature' in a present-day physiological theory would indicate that a portion of physics was being systematically presupposed in the physiological theory. The significance of such an occurrence is that, in asserting that a portion of physics has been *presupposed*, we may be asserting that a number of statements of, say, thermodynamics are being assumed in the physiological theory—in the sense that a *wholly explicit* deduction of testable hypotheses mentioning temperature and comprised in the physiological theory would involve the explicit use of some thermodynamical statements as premises.

In practice, of course, explicit deductions of the kind just alluded to are rarely formulated. In fact, failure to make such deductions, and thus to establish the warrant with which a putative prediction purports to be relevant to the testing of a theory, is just one of the most frequently encountered ways in which current theories fall short of full formalization.

This failure to spell out presupposed statements whose explicit formulation would be required for explicit deductions constitutive of the theory's predictions and explanations is a failure that no doubt is sometimes due to the theoretician's awareness of technical difficulties involved in spelling them out. But such failure is also frequently due just to the theoretician's ignorance of what his theory does presuppose in this sense. To the extent that such an ignorance obtains, of course, will the theory's presuppositions be unexamined and unevaluated; and to the extent that they are unevaluated, our confidence in the theory's adequacy must be qualified. The risks taken in accepting or rejecting such a theory when we make inductive decisions is one determinant of what has been called the *cost* of the theory (cf. my article "The Scientist *Qua* Scientist Makes Value Judgments").

Clearly, when there is knowledge that the material being systematically presupposed in a theory *itself* derives from a relatively well-confirmed body of statements and a relatively well-explicated region of inquiry, say, thermodynamics, our anxiety about the adequacy of our presuppositions is not going to be our most pressing worry. However, we are usually not so fortunate in the material our theory requires us to presuppose. Usually, the issues of weighing the cost of laboriously making presuppositions explicit, and of evaluating this against the possible loss risked by *not* doing so, may become a poignant concern of the methodologically self-conscious scientist or philosopher of science.

All of what has been said so far about the systematic presupposition of portions of "outside" disciplines in partial formalization, applies with equal if not greater force where the material presupposed cannot cogently be construed as indigenous to some other *scientific* area—when, rather, it is constituted of prescientific "common sense" or "common knowledge." Here, it is doubtful that even explicit formulation of commonsensical presuppositions, when they are involved in a theory, will enable us adequately to evaluate the theory's acceptability since the concepts involved are likely to be vague or ambiguous. Yet any reflective reading of social-science theorizing will reveal the considerable frequency with which presupposition of common-sense lore of just this questionable character occurs.

b) *Quasi-deduction.* We shall designate as *quasi-deduction* any putative inference in a theory that purports to be deductively elaborating such theories (the clues that such claims are being made may often be found in the theorist's use of terms such as 'predicting,' 'explaining,' 'setting forth implications,' etc.), but that *fails* to meet the requirements for being a deduction. Such failure usually stems from neglecting, deliberately eschewing, or being unable to make explicit all of the statements requisite as premises, as well as neglecting or being unable to make explicit all of the rules and steps required in arriving at the conclusion. In this sense of 'quasi-deduction,' it is clear that the technique of *systematic presupposition*, described in *a* above, will usually exemplify quasi-deduction as well. But there is one additional factor to notice here. Quasi-deduction in a theory is not confined solely to the implicit assumption of *nonindigenous* material as premises. It is frequently the case that the statements omitted in quasi-deductive inferences are ones indigenous to the theory.

Again, insofar as quasi-deduction characterizes a theory, that theory will fall short of full formalization. Problems in evaluating the adequacy of this type of partial formalization are of the kind already discussed. Here, too, the reflective theorizer's actual decisions concerning adequacy will be based on assessments of the *cost* involved in making such assumptions explicit against the *loss* that may result from not doing so.

c) *Relative primitives.* In the two immediately preceding subsections we have considered partial formalization as a concomitant of the absence of fully explicit deductions. Here, attention will be focused not on problems of suppressed *statements*, but on problems of concept formation in theories that are not fully formalized. We are interested here in the rationale or justification of the *concepts* that occur in a partially formalized theory.

In such theories we may distinguish three (out of the several) techniques or modes of concept presentation or concept introduction.

1. Concepts may be introduced by explicit definition or some equivalent of explicit definition.
2. Concepts may be introduced through some specification, *in* the theory, that yields a sufficient condition for their application.
3. Concepts may be *presented*, not explicated in the modes of 1 and 2, as relative primitives.

Use of the technique of explicit definition in partially formalized theories will ordinarily differ from its use in fully formalized theories only insofar as no set of terms will be exhibited as *the* primitives of the partially formalized theory; hence, no set may be designated as *the* basic or *the* ineliminable set in favor of which *all* other terms may be eliminated.

Statements of a theory that specify a sufficient condition for something's being a thing of a given kind also yield a sufficient condition for the application of the term or concept that indicates the kind. Thus, the statement 'If an animal suckles its young then it is a mammal' not only specifies a sufficient condition for something's being a mammal, but also, of course, furnishes a criterion (if it is a true statement) sufficient for correct applications of the term 'mammal.'

It should be noted that specification of a sufficient condition for a term's application does not fully determine the usage of that term or give its "full meaning." In particular, the very same theory may contain a number of different statements yielding a number of *different* sufficient conditions (none of which need be necessary) for a given term's application. Thus, a theory may comprise the statement 'If an organism has a backbone then it is an animal,' and also, the statement 'If an organism is warm-blooded then it is an animal.' Each of these statements partially determines the usage of the term 'animal'; in a sense, both, taken together, more fully determine the usage than either does alone, but neither separately nor together do they completely determine the usage of the term. Yet such terms (i.e., terms like 'animal') appear to hold promise of eventually being susceptible to full explicit definition in the theory, and therefore, we might well be wary of projecting *ultimately primitive* status to them.

Finally, there will usually occur in partially formalized theories, terms that are not introduced in either of the two ways just mentioned. We shall label such terms, if they are indigenous, *relative primitives*. In so doing, we do not, of course, intend to suggest that the theoretician is utterly in the dark about their meanings. For he will have some clue as to their usage when, for example, a merely *necessary* condition of their use is specified (i.e., he will, in such a case, at least know a criterion for the *inapplicability* of the term to objects to which the term does *not* apply). Similarly, even when a statistically-correlated condition is specified he will have some notion of the "probability" that the term is applicable to some given entity. Indeed, should neither a necessary nor correlated condition be given in the theory for some relative primitive we would still not be forced to construe it as a "meaningless" term, for the term may well have some other ("ordinary-usage") clarity wholly antecedent to its occurrence in the theory.

The important point, however, is that in a theory that has not been fully formalized, the status of terms not introduced by techniques such as those mentioned above, is not automatically that of primitives. Such terms may only be counted as *presumptively* . . . or *tentatively* . . . primitive.

Such theories are, in fact, constantly being modified. A part of a theory that at one time may have occupied a pivotal place in the information on hand about the theory's subject matter can, with the continual acquisition of new knowledge, come to occupy a merely derivative place in a corrected version of the theory. Accordingly, terms that at one time function as primitive, can, at another, be supplanted in this role by different terms, and in a reformulated version of a theory, assume a nonprimitive status. Thus, the ostensible "primitives," e.g., those so regarded for purposes of simplicity assessments of partially formalized theory, might well be construed as only relatively or tentatively primitive. Any simplicity assessments made on this basis would, consequently, be regarded as equally tentative.

d) *How far to formalize*. The rudimentary catalog just completed, of some aspects of partial formalization, will perhaps suffice to indicate problems a *theory* of partial formalization would have to solve. Of course these aspects of partial formalization (as well as the considerations of theoretic and nontheoretic systems that have preceded) "lift and drop a question" on our plates: Given the task of constructing a theory, the *full* formalization of which is not sensibly to be attempted in social science, *to what extent* ought the social scientists attempt to formalize that theory?

The range of possible partial formalizations is vast. As noted above, a theory may be considered formalized to some extent when even *one* putatively deductive connection has been exhibited among its statements, or when the usage of even *one* of its concepts has been partially determined in some explicit fashion. From this extreme to the opposite one of an *almost* completed elaboration of a theory as a deductive system, the theoretician may well have tremendous leeway in the extent to which he may, himself, decide to formalize. What, if any, are rational bases for a decision in this regard? Unfortunately, having raised and dropped this question, we must admit at once to having no wholly satisfactory answer.

Simple answers like 'The scientist should formalize as much as he possibly can,' and pat answers like 'The scientist should formalize as much as it is fruitful to' seem obviously wrong—the first because it is misleading, the second because it is trivial and by itself yields no basis for making a decision.

'Formalize as much as you can' might be sound advice if, e.g., the *only* goal of the scientist were the achievement of the most rigorous possible formulation of his theories. However, he is equally, if not more, concerned with a plurality of other goals, among them prediction, control, and the experimental testing of his theories. Attempts to achieve great rigor in the formulation of a theory may conflict with the achievement of some of these other goals. Furthermore, at a given stage of a theory's development, insistence on great rigor may be stultifying; its premature achievement may even tend to constrict inquiry. Finally, the disproportionate allocation of scientific energies available to this one facet of the scientific enterprise might result in the neglect of other equally important aspects of that enterprise. Of course, these strictures apply pre-eminently to the scientist who must be the initial formulator of scientific theory. They do not apply to the philosopher or logician who may be interested in the different task of rigorously reformulating theories.

In this light, we would not dispute the second dictum, 'Formalize as much as it is fruitful to.' However, to assume that the question 'To what extent shall we formalize?' has been thereby answered is obviously to beg the question. For patently our problem *is* just what constitutes a fruitful degree of formalization at any stage of a theory's development.

It is clear that the nonexistence of an adequate criterion for deciding what constitutes the appropriate degree of formalization has not heretofore had the effect of grinding to a halt theoretical activity in the empirical sciences. In the absence of an explicit rational criterion, theorizers have, in fact, made the requisite decisions consciously or unconsciously, haphazardly or after great reflection; and somehow, of course, the various disciplines have got on. What needs to be emphasized is that these decisions are now perforce made in an essentially intuitive manner, and that consequently we are confronted with an aspect of scientific method, of not inconsiderable importance, that is itself scientifically "out of control."

Elementary considerations concerning partial formalization have been adduced to indicate some of the problems to be solved in applying simplicity criteria to partially formalized theories. In the course of these considerations we have tried at the same time to indicate that another nonevidential criterion, namely *cost*, will also be likely to impinge on such considerations.

USES OF

THEORETICAL FORMULATIONS

AND OBJECTIVITY

3

11. Ideal types and idealizations

In Chapter 2 some of the main methodological problems of the construction of theories and other theoretical formulations in social science were introduced. In this chapter we shall examine uses, and certain problems connected with uses, of theoretical formulations of social science.

Among the formulations discussed in Chapter 2, a favorite of social scientists has been "typologies"—in particular, a kind of typology that features *idealizations* or *ideal types* among its concepts. (Max Weber's important studies of these concepts have, patently, been very influential.)

The discussion of ideal types will provide us with an excellent means of effecting the transition from the nature of formulations in social science to their uses. We shall address ourselves first to the surprisingly complex problem of what kinds of theoretical formulations are constituted by ideal-typical systems. But however complex idealizations may be, and however important or fascinating their effect upon social-science theorizers, we shall find that they still do not constitute a kind of theoretical formulation different from those discussed in Chapter 2. The importance conferred upon ideal types stems especially from the claims that have been made (by Weber and others) concerning the uses of ideal types in theorizing.[1] Accordingly, our discussion will center upon three questions: (*a*) What precisely are ideal types? (*b*) What

[1] Weber made rather uncharacteristically vague and conflicting claims about both the nature and uses of ideal types. Some of his assertions suggest that ideal types are systems of concepts, that is, nontheoretic formulations; others suggest that they are systems of statements, which would imply that they were theoretic formulations. Again, he makes assertions that indicate their use is merely heuristic—that they are not, themselves, susceptible to confirmation or disconfirmation; but he also claims that they belong to the context of validation or justification rather than to the context of discovery when he asserts that they are *methodologically* indispensable in the construction of social-science theory (see his article listed in bibliography).

function are ideal types supposed to have in social science? (*c*) Do they fulfill this function?

Let us begin by recalling the general characterization of typological systems. Those typological systems not simply assimilable to classificational schemata consist rather of some specification of a universe of discourse, an *ordering* relation (or relations) that establishes some ordering of the members of the specified universe of discourse, and an additional set of concepts (frequently polar concepts) designating certain distinguished members in the ordered universe of discourse.

Now, as was indicated above, some claims made for ideal types are obscure about whether an ideal type is to be construed as a *term* (or *concept*) essentially designatory in character (like 'cat') or as a nonanalytic *statement* essentially assertorial in character (like 'The cat is on the mat'). We are not, for the moment, at all concerned with the ideal aspect of the ideal type. The question we are now concerned with arises regardless of any ideal character of the concept, that is, it arises even if the concept *does* designate something (or if we construe the ideal type as a statement, even if there happens to be something extant that the statement describes).

The crucial ambiguity (and it may be found in Weber's own original analysis) regarding the logical character (as concept or statement) of ideal types seems to have had some mischievous effects on a generation of social theorizers. The confusions found in the literature do not arise from the inability of the theorizers to grasp the notion of the usefulness of "ideals," i.e., the usefulness of a nondesignative term (or of a sentence that is not descriptive of anything extant). Rather, those confusions stem, as we shall see, from the muddle that persists about whether an ideal type is a sentence or a term.

This muddle is, in fact, serious, because sentences and terms perform quite disparate functions in theoretical formulations. Consequently, any attempt to ascertain how well, or even whether, ideal types perform their function, is likely to fail if we do not have the crucial information giving their logical character as term or sentence.

There appear, then, to be two main uses, or kinds of application, of terms like 'ideal type,' 'ideal-typical construct,' or sometimes simply 'idealization,' in science. They are ones in which: (*a*) what is referred to is a *predicate* (primitive or defined by primitive predicates) in some typological system; (*b*) the referent is a statemental expression, disguised or undisguised, and *contingent* (i.e., empirically disconfirmable).

With respect to the first of these uses, 'ideal type' refers to a *predicate*—for example, 'perfect competition,' 'open society,' 'perfectly elastic body,' 'ideal gas,' 'Communist society,' etc.—that occurs in a conceptual system and that designates no actual entity. In a system of fully metricized concepts an ideal type or idealization is employed in talk about what *would* (if it *did* exist) exemplify extreme values of some variable ranging over the system's universe of discourse. For example, the concept *ideal gas* designates gases, or gaseous states, in which both the volumes and the masses of molecules assume the extreme value, zero.

In nonmetrical ordered systems the idealizations are frequently construed as applicable to extreme putative instances in the universe of discourse (e.g., 'perfect competition,' 'sacred society'). It should be noted that our concern here is not with the genesis, the cause of or reason for, a theorist's coming to distinguish some potential member of the universe of discourse through use of an ideal-typological concept. We are not concerned (as was Weber) with whether the theorist comes by his notion (his "picturization") by "a one-sided accentuation of and abstraction from" the characteristics of actually observed entities. Our concern is with the logical character of idealizations and their methodological uses. In this latter respect, concepts that happen to be idealizations have, as we shall see, no special *methodological* role—regardless of the *heuristic* or suggestive value they may have in leading theorists to form hypotheses or frame theories about related phenomena. In particular, Weber's historically influential injunction to use idealizations as bases or standards of comparison with actual entities, and to use the results of such comparisons as guides in theory construction, may be seen as a suggestion in heuristics (belonging to the context of discovery) rather than as a methodological suggestion.

We have still to consider a second major usage of 'idealization.' This usage, in which the idealization is a nonanalytic statemental expression, is of particular interest to us. Two related problems arise here: (*a*) accounting for the fact that such idealizations may have explanatory power in science; (*b*) the fact that the methodological uses of such idealizations in the social sciences usually have been quite unsuccessful in helping to furnish explanations while their uses in the physical sciences have often been entirely successful in this respect. In examining these points below we shall employ the terms 'idealization' and 'ideal type' without further qualification to refer to the third kind of expression (i.e., nonanalytic sentences).

Among the social sciences few appear to have achieved the degree of sophistication and rigor in the employment of idealizations achieved by certain branches of economics; this is evidenced in, say, price equilibrium theory by the use of terms such as 'perfect competition.' Accordingly, in contrasting use of idealizations in the social sciences with their use in the nonsocial sciences, we shall not be treating social sciences unfairly by selecting an example from economics to represent the relevant achievements. Let us begin, then, by considering how such an idealization functions in economic theory.

Even a brief perusal of the appropriate literature makes it clear that an ideal-typological expression of economic theory, for example, 'perfect competition,' does not usually occur as an unexplicated primitive predicate in theoretical formulations. Such an idealization, for instance, shares with such ideal concepts of physics as 'the mathematical pendulum,' 'the frictionless engine,' 'the perfectly elastic impact,' 'the ideal gas,' etc., the important characteristic of being simply a convenient shorthand technique for referring to a rather complex set of connected conditions, or for representing the set of statements that describe such conditions. That this is their function in modern economic theory is evidenced by the way in which, say, the concept 'perfect competition' is almost always introduced into theoretical discussions—through some device equivalent to definition, the *definiens* being a set of statements presumably describing just the necessary and sufficient conditions for the occurrence of perfect competition.

Indeed, it is often the case that a sentence containing 'perfect competition' is introduced in a manner sufficiently definitional to reveal it as dispensable in favor of statements not containing the term, but rather, describing the definitory conditions of perfect competition. Thus, such definitory statements may well contain terms like 'perfect knowledge,' 'perfectly accessible market,' and 'economically rational individual'; and they may be logically connected with statements containing terms like 'marginal cost,' 'marginal satisfaction,' or 'price equilibrium.' (Some of these terms also may constitute ideal-type constructs, and in a more fully ramified or articulated theory they too could be eliminated in favor of patterns of definitory expressions in strict analogy, with one or more of the means we have already discussed.)

The point to note about all of this is simply that just as in physical-science theories ideal terms like 'frictionless engine' or 'ideal gas' may be defined by certain sentential expressions, and hence, are eliminable in favor of these, so too in economics a term such as 'perfect competition' is definable and eliminable. Such terms are seen to be a convenient sort of shorthand employed to represent, and thus avoid using, sets of relatively complex statements. It must also be noted that, from a purely logical or syntactical point of view (e.g., from the viewpoint of the logical form or structure of idealization statements), there is *no* way of distinguishing an idealization from a nonidealization. And this is as much the case for the quite respectable idealizations of physical science as it is for economic idealizations—whose credentials we may now proceed to scrutinize.

The distinctive character of contingent sentential idealizations must be sought in the *semantic* (i.e., the referential) or in the *pragmatic* (i.e., the functional) aspect of their occurrence, if, as we have seen, those characteristics are not purely formal or syntactical.

Semantically, the outstanding characteristic of idealizations is that they literally describe nothing—there is no entity, process, or state of affairs to which the idealization stands in designatory or descriptive relation. This is, of course, the reason they are called 'idealizations.'

But this is by no means the end of the matter. In dealing with the idealizations of theoretic formulations we are dealing with lawlike generalizations—with statements whose logical form is that of a universal conditional. We may represent such conditionals in standard form by the expression that follows on the next page.

$$(x) \; [fx \supset gx]$$

This may be read: 'for any entity x, if x has the characteristic f then it has the characteristic g' (where f and g may be characteristics or properties of any degree of complexity).

Now a universally generalized conditional statement can be said to *succeed in describing something* only if a certain corresponding *existential* statement is true—the statement, namely, that there *is* something such that that thing is characterized by f. This may be symbolized by the following expression.

$$(\exists x) \quad fx$$

It should be noticed that the failure of this corresponding existential statement to be true does *not* make the universal generalization itself false; it does mean though, that the universal generalization fails to describe. Universal generalizations (e.g., 'All unicorns have horns') may be true even though there is no instance of what they purport to describe.

But logically, there are *two* kinds of universal generalization that fail to describe, one of which is the type we have just been discussing— the type whose failure to describe is reflected in and follows from the falsity of some corresponding existential statement. The other kind of nondescribing universal generalizations are those which are analytic— that is to say, statements that are true independently of any extra-linguistic facts. Such statements fail to describe not because the universe happens not to exhibit what they, so to speak, mention, but rather, because they do not purport to describe anything at all—not even ideal conditions or situations.

An analytic statement has no empirical content; which means (as we shall see in detail shortly) that it has no explanatory or predictive power whatever. Analytic statements cannot be either confirmed or disconfirmed by empirical findings; their truth-value is determined a priori—without recourse to extralinguistic investigation. Confusing the statements constitutive of contingent idealizations with analytic statements has perhaps been one of the main sources of the mix-up concerning idealizations in the social sciences. The rationale for the use of contingent idealizations must lie in their explanatory or predictive powers; analytic, in contrast to any contingent statements, on the other hand, have no such powers. All contingent idealizations must be susceptible to disconfirmation; analytic statements cannot be disconfirmed.

Idealizations do purport to describe "possible" states of affairs. Their occurrence in theories is distinguishable from the occurrence of a theory's other contingent statements by the fact that we have initially, or we have come ultimately to acquire, overwhelming empirical evidence against the existence of the things such idealizations purport to describe. How idealizations can, in spite of this, *have* explanatory or predictive power is a puzzle.

But this puzzle is solvable. If it were the explanatory or predictive power of *analytic* statements that confronted us, the puzzle of how such statements could have explanatory or predictive power would be unsolvable, since it would involve an obvious inconsistency.

So far we have examined only the syntactical and semantical aspects of idealizations. We must turn, now, to *pragmatic* considerations. And indeed, since a good deal of economic theory appears on close scrutiny to *be* idealization, such study may provide us with a key to the assessment of the current explanatory status of much of economic theory itself.

Proponents of the use of idealizations in social science—in particular, in economics—have argued for them on at least two distinct (in fact, apparently conflicting) grounds. Some (like Weber) have argued that because the social sciences are radically different from the physical sciences, the use of ideal types is an indispensable explanatory device in the methodology of the social sciences. Others have argued, in effect, that a warrant for the explanatory use of idealizations in social science is to be found precisely in the successful precedent of idealizations in physical science. What both proponents appear to have in common, however, is the view that idealizations are justified in science by their relevance to explanation; and it is this last claim that we too shall examine in assessing their role in social science.

To begin, let us consider in at least an elementary way what a *scientific explanation* is.[2] An explanation, generally speaking, is an answer to the question 'Why?' In ordinary discourse there are at least two distinct senses in which we ask such a question. We sometimes employ 'Why?' in the sense of 'for what motive?' Thus, when we ask a friend why he throttled his wife, we are usually asking what motivated him to do so. However, we also use 'Why?' in the quite different sense of 'How did it come about that . . . ?' Here, we do not make any imputation of motivation. We are asking 'How come?' in the sense of 'What sort of things brought it about?' or 'What conditions resulted in this?' or even more pedantically, 'In accordance with what natural regularities did this phenomenon occur?' Thus, when we ask, 'Why do clouds produce rain?' few, if any, of us are asking, 'What motives do the clouds have for producing rain?' In the days when men may have been somewhat more prone to committing fallacies of anthropomorphism than they now are, no doubt the original sense of 'Why?' *was* motivational. With the advent of the age of science, however, we have presumably become more sophisticated; and when the question 'Why?' is construed as a demand for a scientific explanation, the second or 'How come?' interpretation is the appropriate one.

[2] What follows is, perforce, a quite rudimentary sketch of a complex topic in the philosophy of science—a topic, moreover, that continues to reveal its complexity in discussions currently going on in the literature of the field. The sophistication of these recent discussions make it especially important to emphasize the rudimentary character of the treatment given in this section. For penetrating analyses of the topic and of points currently at issue, see bibliography for Hempel's "Deductive-Nomological vs. Statistical Explanation" and "Problems of Concept and Theory Formation in the Social Sciences," and works by Nagel, Grünbaum, and Sellars.

When a young child asks, 'Why did the balloon burst?' he may be asking for the balloon's motives. When *we* seriously ask the same question we are, on the contrary, usually asking for a scientific explanation. Suppose, then, someone should answer that the balloon burst because it was held near a flame and became very hot. If we are reflective, this answer may not satisfy us, and we may go on to ask: 'What does the balloon's getting hot have to do with its bursting?' And now, our informant might point out that when gases, such as the air contained in the balloon, are heated, they expand, and the increased pressure of the expanding air against the sides of the balloon caused it to burst.

These additional comments, containing at least implicit employment of lawlike generalizations, would have provided us with an answer that, despite its crudeness, contained most of the kinds of constituents required for a full-fledged scientific explanation.

The formal structure of a scientific explanation of some specific event has three parts: first, a statement E describing the specific event to be explained; second, a set of statements C_1 to C_n describing specific relevant circumstances that are antecedent to, or otherwise causally correlated with, the event described by E; third, a set of lawlike statements L_1 to L_n, universal generalizations whose import is roughly, 'Whenever events of the kind described by C_1 through C_n take place, then an event of the kind described by E takes place.'

In order for these three sets of statements actually to constitute an explanation of the event, they must fulfill at least two conditions: first, the E statement must be deducible from the C and L statements together, but not from either set alone, and second, the C and L statements must be true. A skeleton outline of a scientific explanation looks like the following.

$$L_1 \ldots L_n$$
$$C_1 \ldots C_n$$
$$\overline{\therefore\ E}$$

It is of some interest to note that the logical structure of a scientific *explanation* is identical with that of a scientific *prediction*, the only difference between them being the purely pragmatic one of the temporal vantage point of the inquirer. In the case of explanation, we have, so to speak, our E (the E is about a past event relative to the scientist's present temporal vantage point), and seek the appropriate L's and C's under which to subsume it; in the case of prediction, we already have our L's and C's and seek instead an E (about an event not of the scientist's past) that they imply. It follows from these considerations that *we have an explanation for an event if, and only if* (from a different temporal vantage point), *we could have predicted it.* There are some important qualifications and elaborations to be made on these considerations, however, and we shall return to them in section 12.

There are two other comments about explanation or prediction that are germane to our discussion. First, the use of lawlike statements (whose logical form is that of universal generalizations) is an indispensable prerequisite to the accomplishment of either. Second, and associated with this, we can now say with precision what we mean when we assert that it is *a function* of scientific theories to explain or predict: Scientific theories provide the lawlike statements constitutive of them to explanatory or predictive arguments of the sort just outlined.

We may now return to the primary problem of this section—the explanatory or predictive efficacy of idealizations. Most students of the topic agree that idealizations have such an efficacy in some theories of physical science. But the import of this agreement is that it is not the idealization alone that has explanatory power, but the idealization within the context of the physical theory in which it is, in fact, embedded—or alternatively, that it is that theory itself which, in containing the idealization, comes to have this explanatory power.

There are at least three special conditions that characterize and help account for the successful use of idealizations in, say, physics, and it will be helpful to see as clearly as possible what these conditions are. The first is indicated by the fact that in physics the idealization is always subsumed under, i.e., is deducible from, more general laws or more comprehensive theories for which latter, in turn, *independent* confirming evidence already exists. This means that we are thereby furnished with evidence for the truth of the contingent idealized formulations—evidence achieved, of course, independently of the actualization of the ideal's (so far as we know) unactualizable conditions. If we had no such independent evidence there would simply be no way of discriminating between the idealizations we find acceptable, such as 'the perfectly elastic impact,' and those we reject as unacceptable, such as the 'space-warp drive.'

The second special property of successful idealizations in physics has to do with the manner in which they are deduced within physical theories. In such theories the idealization may be arrived at by letting variables (which occur in comprehensive formulations that have already been independently confirmed) take on certain extreme values. Thus, for example, the Boyle-Charles law for ideal gases is arrived at within the more comprehensive kinetic theory by giving the extreme value of zero to the variables for molecular volume and molecular attraction.

An important correlate of this is that such theories also give us precise ways of comparing the actual with the ideal by giving us precise ways of characterizing and testing for situations that deviate from the ideal by precisely specifiable gradations.

The third special property of idealizations in physics centers on the *operational clarity* of the concepts that are involved in those idealizations. Metric variable concepts like *mass, temperature, volume, pressure, distance,* etc., all of which, at extreme values, may become constituents of physical idealizations, have been given relatively precise operational interpretations for many of their actually exemplified values. This enables the physical scientist to judge with some assurance those concrete situations to which they would or would not apply, as well as the "extent" to which they might apply.

It is the possession of some or all of the three properties just mentioned that Carl Hempel may have in mind in his "Problems of Concept Formation in the Social Sciences" (see bibliography), when he distinguishes between what he calls *theoretical idealizations* and *intuitive idealizations*. An intuitive idealization may meet the conditions delineated above in passages on the syntactical and semantical aspects of the problem; but such an intuitive idealization cannot achieve the status of a theoretical idealization, and thus cannot be cogently judged to have achieved any significant explanatory or predictive power, unless it also takes on all three of the special properties just outlined.

Leaving physics, we can now turn to an assessment of the claims of explanatory power, which in economics are put forward as justification for the use of idealizations such as 'perfect competition.'

Consider, for example, those economic idealizations that incorporate the idealizing assumption of *economically rational behavior*—the assumption that Joan Robinson, in her *Economics of Imperfect Competition* (p. 15), formulates in a forthright way as: "Each individual acts in a sensible manner. . . ." We might expect that a general theory of social behavior or a general theory of social action would, were it a viable theory, have variables of behavior such that descriptions of the sort of rational behavior Mrs. Robinson seems to have in mind could be *derived* by letting those variables take on extreme values. Such a comprehensive theory of social action would, in short, subsume economically rational behavior (or sensible behavior) as a special case. Unfortunately, no such comprehensive theory seems at present to be available.[3]

On this score, then, and at this stage of our knowledge, one could not admit idealizations embodying the concept (or disguised sentence) indicated by 'economically rational man' to the status of theoretical idealizations; this would also hold true for 'perfect competition.' But there is no reason for holding that such idealizations will never achieve this very useful methodological status.

The questions initiating this examination of nonanalytic, sentential idealizations may now be answered quite briefly. Such idealizations comprise universal generalizations (lawlike sentences) that may be true even though they "fail to describe anything." Their methodological (as distinct from their heuristic) task is to function explanatorily, and when they succeed in doing so (e.g., as in physics) it is through their subsumption under more general, independently evidenced theories which furnish them (as well as other statements) to the explanations in which they do figure. Their failure to achieve significant explanatory

---

[3] *Pace* Parsons.

power in the social sciences is a result of the paucity in such disciplines of the requisite general theory.

2. Explanatory and predictive systematizations, rational foresight and rational hindsight

a) *Explanatory arguments*. In section 11 we discussed sentential idealizations in science in order to effect the transition from the treatment of the *nature* of various scientific formulations to a treatment of their *uses*. In that discussion we had occasion in preliminary fashion to consider what constitutes scientific explanation and prediction, and concluded that both scientific explanation and prediction are deductive systematizations of statements. These should, in fact, properly be construed as *arguments* in which the conclusion is the sentence *E*, describing the event to be explained (the *explanandum*), while the premises (the *explanans*) are the sentences—the lawlike sentences L_1 to L_n and particular-circumstance sentences C_1 to C_n—that purport to do the explaining. The argument is such, moreover, that the sentences of the *explanans* are supposed to imply logically the *explanandum*.

Note that although a *theory* is also a deductive systematization of its constituent statements, and although one of the important uses of theories is to "lend" their constituent lawlike statements to explanatory arguments, the latter may still be distinguished from theories. In particular, the lawlike statements that are part of the *explanans* of every explanatory argument need by no means have their origin in any one theory.

Again, the *explanandum* descriptive of some specific event (and thus, a singular rather than a general statement) will not ordinarily be counted as a constituent of any scientific theory (cf. Braithwaite's *Scientific Explanation*, listed in the bibliography).

As was indicated in section 11, a scientist may employ a given explanatory argument either to explain or to predict the event described by its *explanandum*. Whether his use of the argument will constitute an explanation or a prediction will depend on whether that use occurs at a time earlier than the event described by the *explanandum* (in which case he is using it to effect a prediction of that event) or subsequent to the time of the *explanandum* (in which case he is employing it to effect an explanation of the event). The explanatory argument itself is unchanged by, and independent of, the time at which (or for that matter, the scientist by whom) it is used. This characteristic of explanatory arguments is sometimes referred to as 'the symmetry of scientific explanation and prediction'; it is likewise being referred to when the claim is made that no systematization could serve as a scientific explanation of an event unless it could also have served as a prediction—and conversely.

Among explanatory arguments it is also sometimes useful to distinguish those which are *retro-dictive* from those which are *pro-dictive*. A retro-dictive explanatory argument is one whose *explanandum* describes an event that is temporally antecedent to any events described by the particular-circumstance statements of its *explanans*. A pro-dictive explanatory argument is one whose *explanandum* describes an event temporally posterior to at least one of the particular-circumstance statements of the *explanans*. It should be clear that the pro-dictivity or retro-dictivity of an explanatory argument—which depends upon temporal relations between *explanandum* and some statements of the *explanans*—does not determine whether a given use is a predictive or an explanational use of that explanatory argument; for this latter fact depends *only* on a temporal relation between the *explanandum* and the date on which the use occurs (regardless of the dates of the *explanans* events).

A little reflection will show that the kind of symmetry characterizing explanational and predictive uses does not, in general, characterize retro-diction and pro-diction. No explanatory argument that is one of these latter two types can function as the other of the two. The dates of *explanandum* and *explanans* determine immutably and eternally into which of these two latter types a given explanatory argument will fall. In recent literature on the topic of explanation, the difference between predictive or explanational *uses* of explanatory arguments on the one hand, and on the other hand, the retro-dictive or pro-dictive *character* of an explanatory argument, has been overlooked, resulting in confusion and fallacious argument. This has been especially true of a spate of discussions which appear to have argued erroneously from the failure of symmetry between retro-diction and pro-diction, to a corresponding failure of symmetry between explanational and predictive uses of explanatory arguments. The spate of recent discussions and criticisms of earlier treatments of explanation has, however, had the effect of helping to induce proponents of the symmetry thesis to present us with a more subtle analysis of the complexities of explanatory arguments than had hitherto been vouchsafed (see bibliography for Hempel's "Deductive-Nomological vs. Statistical Explanation" and Grünbaum's "Temporally-Asymmetrical Principles . . .").

Retro-dictive and pro-dictive arguments do not exhaust the possible types of explanatory argument. There are some explanatory arguments whose lawlike sentences comprise only laws of atemporal correlation. Since these arguments contain no laws of succession (i.e., no laws that speak of one kind of event as occurring *later* than another kind), they will clearly not be countable as either type. For in such cases, particular-circumstance sentences of the *explanans* and the *explanandum* statement will be either undated or identically dated.

Indeed, some writers choose not to construe this last kind of argument as *explanatory* at all. They give as grounds for this view the thesis that explanations must be causal in character, and that since the notion of cause essentially involves temporal succession, it follows that arguments containing only laws of atemporal correlation (e.g., the Boyle-Charles law, Ohm's law, Archimedes' law of the lever, etc.) cannot qualify as causal arguments, and hence, not as explanatory. Proponents of this viewpoint do not, of course, deny that laws of atemporal correlation are just as much laws of nature or just as much scientific laws as are laws of succession.

The fact is that the idea of cause appears to have become subordinate in modern science to the idea of *lawlike regularity* and there appears to be no very good reason for withholding the term 'explanatory argument' from an argument that fulfills all of the conditions for such but that contains only laws of atemporal correlation. If we take this notion of explanatory argument as the generic one, then causal explanations may be construed as a subspecies. In any case, whether the term 'explanatory argument' is withheld or not seems less important than being clear about the ground of the possible distinction.

b) Rational forecast and rational hindsight. Perhaps enough has been said to indicate that the terms 'prediction' and 'explanation' are technical terms belonging to scientific methodology. Yet they share with such terms as 'work' in physics, and 'fish' in biology, an intimate relationship with terms having a currency (but perhaps not as precise a meaning) in ordinary nontechnical discourse. For example, as the term 'prediction' is used in ordinary discourse (and even in the "ordinary" discourse of scientists), its meaning clearly differs from the technical sense of 'prediction' delineated above as the meaning of 'work' in ordinary discourse differs from 'work' in physics.

What 'prediction' refers to in ordinary usage is, in fact, not an argument, but rather, any statement about some event future to its formulation or utterance. In the context of ordinary usage, to "make a prediction" corresponds only to the employment of the *explanandum* of a full-fledged scientific prediction. It is clear that if the technical and nontechnical senses of the term are not sharply distinguished—especially in talk about "the nature of prediction"—opportunities for confusion become rife.

In what follows we shall employ the term 'prediction' in its technical sense; when we have occasion to refer to a *single* statement about the future we shall employ the locution 'predictive statement.' It should be especially noted that the assertion, true of predictions, that the only difference between prediction and explanation is the temporal vantage point of the employer of the explanatory argument, makes no sense at all if applied to *predictive statements*. This is not, of course, to say that scientists have no interest in predictive statements. It is obvious that such statements, quite apart from their potential or actual occurrences in explanatory arguments, figure prominently in the social sciences where forecasting, as a substitute for prediction, continues to play an extremely important role among the scientist's activities.

The social scientist's uses of predictive statements are made (in the absence of the systematizing functions that would be afforded by the availability of full theories with their accompanying panoplies of laws) primarily to achieve what might be called rational foresight (or for post-dictive statements, rational hindsights).

"Rational foresight" may thus be given a relatively precise meaning: the term applies when we have accepted (or are proposing) a hypothesis about the future and our acceptance is an inductively warranted one. It should be noted that rational foresight is broader than, and embraces, scientific prediction. This is so insofar as accepting a scientific prediction involves accepting a statement (say, the *explanandum*) about the future by accepting as sound an explanatory argument having that statement as a conclusion.

But 'rational foresight' is also more extensive or general than 'scientific prediction,' for it applies to the acceptance of any sufficiently warranted statement about the future—regardless of whether the inductive warrant is given (as in scientific prediction) by a set of well-confirmed sentences that deductively imply the future-statement, or whether we are warranted in accepting the statement on its own, so to speak. This is to say that we are sometimes justified in accepting scientific hypotheses about the future even if the evidence supporting them (i.e., statements adduced in their support) may fail to include any that deductively imply such a hypothesis.[4]

Some important writers hold that rational foresight or forecast should be construed as an employment of a nondeductive argument, one whose premises and form have the character of rendering the conclusion probable, or likely to be true, rather than of guaranteeing the truth of the conclusion on the basis of the truth of its premises (see bibliography for Hempel's "Deductive-Nomological vs. Statistical Explanation," and this article's bibliography as well, for a consideration of this view). On this view there are two types of explanatory argument, one that deductively implies the *explanandum*, and one that merely has the character of supporting the *explanandum* without logically implying it. But there seems to be no very compelling reason either for insisting on speaking of two rather than of only one type of explanatory argument, or for insisting on reserving the term 'explanatory argument' for the deductive type. And, in fact, both these usages appear in the current literature, although we have adopted the latter here.

While the decision about whether or not to refer to foresight or hindsight as a use of explanatory argument may not in itself pose a very important problem, this surely cannot be claimed about the precise meaning of 'support' as it is used in connection with rational foresight or hindsight. For this latter problem itself involves the problem of framing an adequate logic of induction, i.e., a system for choosing among

---

[4] The vulgar notion that *induction* and *deduction* are "opposites" as well as its equally untutored concomitant notions that deduction is "going" from the general to the particular, and induction is "going" from the particular to the general, are not only quite mistaken, but seriously misleading. Not only is deduction not restricted to inference from the general to the particular, but also, induction—which comprises the selection of hypotheses—does frequently involve, as one of its steps, the making of a deduction. There is surely no longer an excuse for repeating such bits of foolish folk-lore "logic."

hypotheses that are variously supported or even for deciding simply that any given hypothesis *is* supported.[5]

One of the reasons for desiring to extend the term 'explanatory argument' so that it covers nondeductive cases in social science has been the paucity of *nonprobabilistic* laws. A nonprobabilistic law claims an exceptionless concomitance of characteristics (i.e., it is a law which claims that given the occurrence of a certain type of characteristic, there will concomitantly occur—without exception—a characteristic of a second type). But few, if any, exceptionless concomitances appear to have been discovered by inquiries in social science. Accordingly, generalizations in social science are usually probabilistic in character. Such generalizations claim only what is compatible with the observation of individual exceptions. Indeed, such assertions refer to no individual cases, but only to classes or sets of individual cases.

Suppose we have a probabilistic or statistical law whose form may be expressed as follows:

> If anyone has a certain characteristic A, then—with a probability of p—he will have the characteristic B.

If this law is appropriately employed in an ostensibly explanatory argument, no conclusion about any specific individual may be deduced. Thus, any such arguments that do purport to be explanatory of individual social phenomena must rest not on a deductive paradigm, but on one in which the statistical or probabilistic premises lend some, but less than conclusive, support to the *explanandum* event (see bibliography for Hempel's "Deductive-Nomological vs. Statistical Explanation" and Salmon's *Logic*).

[5] The problem of analyzing the concept *support sufficient for acceptance of a hypothesis* is patently not restricted to the philosophy of social science. It belongs, rather, to the more general discipline of philosophy of science. Accordingly, though even in this book of restricted scope we shall be touching on the problem of what might be involved in assessing the acceptability of statements, or what might be involved in using the concept 'sufficient support,' we shall not be in a position to give that problem the full-scale consideration appropriate to the more general discipline.

ON THE OBJECTIVITY

OF SOCIAL SCIENCE

4

**13. The
recalcitrance
of social
phenomena
to scientific
Investigation**
For many years the social sciences have been fair game for a
number of critics; and the criticisms leveled have been varied,
ranging from scepticism concerning the activity of social scientists
because "social science isn't really possible," to horror at the activity of social scientists because "too much social knowledge will
endanger man's freedom." This chapter will be concerned with
evaluating some of the more dominant themes sounded by critics
sceptical of the scientific status of social science.

Let us begin by examining the arguments of those who hold that
social phenomena are too *complex* to be scientifically investigated, a
criticism that sometimes begins with the milder claim that social-science
laws, if there are any, can at best be "merely probabilistic." It is sometimes held that the failure of the social scientist to employ nonprobabilistic laws is due to the complexity of phenomena with which
he must deal, in contrast to the presumably less complex phenomena
studied by the social scientist's more fortunate neighbors in other disciplines. Is there anything to this claim?

Actually, it is a rather difficult claim to assess, mainly because
different proponents of it appear to have quite different things in mind
in making it. For example, some critics have alleged not merely the
complexity of social phenomena as a ground for concluding that social
science is, in effect, impossible, but also, the stronger thesis that *all*
science is impossible because of the complexity of *all* phenomena. Not
only is the behavior of human beings too complicated "to be captured"
or accounted for by science according to this far-reaching view, but also,
in the realm of the nonsocial, the intricacies of leaf patterns, the subtle
play of light and shadow in a meadow on a partly cloudy afternoon, the
purling waters of a brook—in fact, *all* phenomena of the physical and
biological realms—must forever, on account of their infinite complexity
and subtlety, elude the "gross, distorting, pigeon-holing" of any scientific

inquiry. It would be well to dispose of this far-reaching thesis before examining similar ones that place only the social sciences in a peculiarly invidious position. As we shall see, both the argument that all science is impossible and the argument that only social science is impossible (on account of the grossness, lack of subtlety, abstractness, or other distortedness of scientific inquiry and its consequent inability to "capture reality") rest in some measure on the same kind of mistake.

a) A *preliminary mistake about science*. The issue in question has to do with what science is, or what it could conceivably purport to do. So elementary that it is difficult to see how it is made at all, the mistake involved consists in assuming that it is the function of science to *reproduce* "reality" and concluding that science is defective from the fact that it accomplishes no such thing. Basically, this error rests on a confusion between a description and what is described. Albert Einstein once remarked, it is not the function of science 'to *give* the taste of the soup.' To be a description of the taste of soup is clearly not to *be* the taste of soup. On reflection there is surely no reason whatever for anyone to suppose that a description of some characteristic of soup should, itself, taste like soup. Yet a muddle just as egregious is involved in disparaging science's alleged failures in this respect. Of course, if we are intelligent and lucky, and employ sensibly the information conveyed by the statements of science, we may be able to put ourselves into the position of tasting soup. But this is, of course, quite different from expecting that the statements of science (the ones *about* the taste of soup) are defective, or somehow fail, because *they* don't taste like soup.

A related and only slightly less egregious confusion about the character and functions of science consists not in the belief that science's function is literally to reproduce the world, but in the belief that the statements of science should convey to us the same, or something like the same, sensations, reactions, responses—in a word, *experiences*—as would be conveyed by an actual confrontation with what those statements describe. It might, of course, be argued that this is a function of art—of poetry or painting—but it seems scarcely tenable that this should be an aim in the formulation of scientific statements; for the very thrall in which experiences so conveyed may hold us might be quite incompatible with, and is surely irrelevant to, our predictive, explanatory, or other systematizing uses of such statements.

Thus, when the charge that "reality is too complex to be captured" by science rests, as it often seems to have rested, on confusion about the statements of science and how they are related to what they describe in the extralinguistic world, then we cannot put credence in that charge. It rests upon a serious, if elementary, error about the nature of science and functions of scientific statements.

b) *The imputation of this failure to social science*. The alleged failure of social science to "capture" (i.e., to reproduce or to be the psychological equivalent of) the delighted chortle of a baby in social play with its parent, the anguished embarrassment of an adolescent, the nuances of social interaction of a board of directors meeting or of a cocktail party, is too often nothing but the failure to distinguish statements and the systematizing uses to which they may be put, from the social phenomena referred to by those statements.

Not all of the arguments from the complexity of social phenomena to the impossibility of social science (or to the impossibility of a social science whose methodology coincides with the rest of the sciences) have had just this patently wrongheaded rationale, however.[1] Another set of arguments for the same conclusion rests on an alleged inability of the scientific method to capture the *uniqueness* of social (or human) phenomena. Since, so the argument runs, it is to the uniqueness of any social event that the social inquirer's interest is turned, and since the method of science is capable of systematizing only by *generalizing* (i.e., by relegating entities to categories or types and describing them by generalizing over all members of such types), it follows that some method other than the scientific (i.e., other than the one presumably followed in the nonsocial sciences) must be employed in the social sciences.

To determine how cogent arguments of this sort are, we must ask ourselves what could be meant by the term 'unique' and its cognates in this context. Now, it is clear that any entity is unique in a *strict* sense if, and only if, it is different from any other entity. But (again, strictly) one entity is different from all others if, and only if, there is no other entity that has exactly the same set of characteristics (i.e., all and only the characteristics) it itself has. Thus, of any two different things *A* and *B*, there will be at least one characteristic that one of them, but not the other, possesses. This not simply a matter of discovered fact; it is a matter of logic, for it is part of what is meant by saying they are *different* or *nonidentical* things.

One upshot of the above remarks is that, strictly speaking, every entity is different from every other entity, i.e., no two entities are identical, for if they were identical they wouldn't be *two*. Consequently, in this strict sense all phenomena, and not merely social-science phenomena, are unique. From this it follows that if the proponents of the uniqueness view were correct, and if the intended sense of uniqueness were the clear, strict one just delineated, then not only social science, but *all* science would be impossible. For obviously, in this sense, every physical phenomenon, every physical entity, is "just as unique" as every social phenomenon or social entity. Accordingly, arguments based on this sense of uniqueness give no support at all to the view that there

---

[1] See, for example P. Winch's *The Idea of a Social Science*, listed in the bibliography. Winch's arguments are, in detail, subtle and profound. In summary, however, they *are* to the effect that because social phenomena, e.g., social behavior, are *rule-governed*, the kind of knowledge appropriate to social inquiry can only be gained by coming to "learn the rules." But coming to learn the rules, in turn, entails knowing the phenomena from the "inside," i.e., *having the experiences* of behaving in conformance with those rules. Despite their unusual subtlety and importance, his arguments are thus also a species of what, if the remarks in the text are cogent, might be called the "reproductive fallacy."

must be a radical divorce between the methodologies of the nonsocial and the social sciences.[2]

c) *Emergentism.* Closely allied to the argument for a radical difference in methodology, but traditionally somewhat more lucidly advanced, has been the argument for *emergence.* Emergentists have often held the more moderate position that *some* social phenomena (and indeed, some physical and biological phenomena), rather than *all* of them, are not amenable to scientific investigation insofar as such investigation is causal. This scepticism is sometimes based on a special thesis—the thesis of absolute emergence—which advances the belief that some events are, in *principle,* unpredictable (i.e., there are events the prediction of which is *logically impossible*), since they are not connected with other events in any lawlike fashion. In contrast, the thesis of *relative* emergence is that, relative to certain circumstances (e.g., our technology or knowledge, or the inaccessibility to observation of phenomena, at a given time), it is not *technically possible* to predict the occurrence of certain events.

Although the thesis of relative emergence is doubtless true, it does not imply that any social phenomena are closed to investigation by means of the scientific method. For the thesis of absolute emergence, a thesis that *does* imply the inapplicability of the scientific method, there appears to be no plausible evidence whatever. It is, in fact, an extraordinarily strong thesis. In order to establish it, a proponent would have to prove not merely that no lawlike hypothesis applying to the putatively emergent event had been formulated, nor even that none would be or would be likely to be formulated in the future, but rather, he would have to prove that *it is logically impossible for any such hypothesis to ever be formulated.* Not only has no proponent of the thesis of absolute emergence produced anything that even begins to approximate such a proof, but it is very difficult to imagine how a proponent could ever go about doing so. To the contrary, the history of science exhibits numerous instances of phenomena for which the status of absolute emergence has been claimed but which have subsequently been shown not to be outside the pattern of lawlike regularity of other events.

d) *Verstehen.* No serious discussion of the various grounds on the basis of which social phenomena have been held *not* amenable to

[2] Unfortunately, proponents of the 'uniqueness' claim have not been limpid in their expositions of what they have intended by the term 'unique.' Perhaps they have meant that social phenomena are unique not only in the standard logical (Leibnizian) sense indicated above, but also in a somewhat stronger sense—an object would be unique not only if no other object had exactly the *same set* of characteristics it had, but if it also had some characteristics that no other object had. But there seems no reason whatever for believing either that all social phenomena are unique, or that no physical phenomena are unique, in this sense, or that the stronger form of uniqueness would be any more recalcitrant to science than the weaker sense. In this respect it should be remembered that the validity or usefulness of a scientific generalization is in no way dependent upon the *number* of entities to which it actually applies (*cf.* section 11 on idealizations).

scientific investigation could reasonably omit mention of the issue of *Verstehen,* or empathic understanding. As in the cases mentioned above, here too we find proponents of the view that the methodology of the social sciences must be radically different from that of the other sciences.

In this case it is especially important to keep the distinctions between methodology and technique, and validation and discovery, clearly in mind. The issue is not whether achieving empathic understanding of some subject of inquiry (presumably by an imaginative act of psychologically "putting oneself into the place of" the subject) is a helpful, fruitful, or indispensable technique for discovering hypotheses, or means for testing hypotheses. The issue is not even whether such techniques of discovery are peculiarly techniques of the social scientist. What is at issue is whether empathic understanding constitutes an indispensable method for the validation of hypotheses about social phenomena. This question had best be considered in two stages: First, in what sense, if any, is *Verstehen* a validational method? Second, is it an indispensable methodological recourse of the social sciences alone?

Concerning the first question, it is clear that some serious and influential students of the methodology of the social sciences (see bibliography for works by Oakeshott, Winch, and Weber) have thought the aim of social inquiry to be a kind of *understanding* of the phenomena investigated, which can be gained or validated by empathic, or empathy-like, or other participatory acts of the investigator. For several proponents of the view, this thesis is connected with the assertion that social activities have a "significance" or "meaning," and that hypotheses about this significance can be validated *through* the empathy of the investigator. In section 14 we shall have something further to say about problems posed by what is termed the 'meaningfulness' of social phenomena. For the present, however, let us assume that meaningfulness is an unproblematic concept and confine our attention solely to the analysis of the empathic part of the current question.

Max Weber and other proponents of the methodological use of empathy have maintained that coming to the kind of understanding required in social science of, say, the phenomenon of religious martyrdom, is through empathy with martyrs. In order really to understand Christian martyrdom, to validate hypotheses about its sociocultural character, to accomplish the requisite task of capturing the "meaning" that martyrdom had for the martyr, we imagine ourselves in the place of, or "recreate" the psychological states of, the martyr—and thus, presumably, come to the requisite understanding and effect the requisite validation. (For Weber and others, not only is this empathic method a means for the social scientist to "capture" the significance of Christian martyrdom, but it is the only, and hence, indispensable, means for doing so. It is, moreover, peculiar to social science by its very nature.)

The above will suffice perhaps to give something of the flavor of the proponents' arguments—which arguments we may now examine. To begin, even if we waive consideration of the vagueness of 'meaningful-ness' and 'understanding' in this context, there is still a residual oddness about this thesis that makes it something less than compelling. The question that arises on reflection is this: What check does the empathizer have on whether his empathic state is veridical (i.e., reliable)? We need not argue against empathy or discard it as a validational step, but clearly, in order to accept some specific empathic act as validational, we must presuppose an investigation establishing the hypothesis that this act is veridical. In short, to provide the empathizer with a reliable basis for accepting or rejecting his hypotheses about the phenomenon he is investigating, we must have established independently that the empathy is sufficiently like the state of which it is an empathy.

But how can we establish independently the reliability of such an empathic act without having had previous knowledge of (i.e., without having previously accepted a hypothesis about the character of) the very psychological state that is the object of empathy? And if we do have this presupposed knowledge (i.e., if we have already accepted a hypothesis about the nature of the target psychological state) what more could be methodologically required? If further confirmation of the investigator's hypotheses about the character of the target psychological state *is* in order, then the logic of the situation just outlined entails that some means are available, independent of empathy, for acquiring it.

A little reflection will show that these considerations answer the second question about empathy posed earlier, as well as the first. The answer to the first question is that if we waive (temporarily) difficulties about such terms as 'meaningfulness' and 'understanding,' it is possible to accept empathy as a validational method in those cases where its veridicalness or reliability has been independently established in such a way as to have made it redundant. The answer to the second question is, therefore, that empathy is *not* an indispensable methodological device of the social sciences. The very logic of its methodological employment precludes this by guaranteeing that there will be independent means for validating the hypotheses its use is intended to validate.

14. The objectivity of social science   *a*) *'Objectivity.'* Closely connected with the view that some peculi-arity of social phenomena precludes using the scientific method to investigate them, is the view that the social sciences cannot achieve "objectivity." The difficulty in assessing this charge, like the difficulties in assessing the charges examined in section 13, is, in part, the obscurity that attends the charge itself. Specifically, it is fre-quently not at all clear what those who level the charge have in mind in their uses of the term 'objectivity.' Before we can properly evaluate the cogency of the charge we must see if it is possible to become clear about some of the appropriate meanings of this key term.

A pivotal source of the confusion that has attended uses of the term 'objectivity' stems from a remarkable ambiguity which 'objective' and its polar-opposite, 'subjective,' have had inflicted on them (in part by a traditional metaphysical view, the apparent popularity and vitality of which is out of all proportion to the number of times it seems to have been discredited in the history of philosophy). The ambiguity involved stems from being unclear about those uses of 'subjective' and 'objective' that mean something very much like 'psychological' and 'nonpsychological' respectively, and those uses of 'subjective' and 'objective' that mean something like 'biased' (or 'error-laden') and 'unbiased' (or 'error-free') respectively.

Now, these *are* quite distinct pairs of meanings, and mixing them up in the controversies that have raged over the status of the social sciences has been an especially fertile source of many of the confusions that haunt the voluminous literature of these controversies. Notice, for example, that if (adopting now the metaphysical position alluded to above) we routinely were to *identify* the referent of 'subjective' in the sense in which the term applies simply to psychological states, with the referent of that term in the sense in which the term is roughly synonymous with 'biased,' then the result of that identification would be that such perfectly useful locutions as 'take an objective approach to' or 'look at from an objective point of view' or 'evaluate objectively,' and many similar locutions, would have to be regarded as gibberish. For on this assumption the locution 'unbiased viewpoint' would be self-inconsistent.

No one has ever demonstrated that the psychological, per se, is identical with the biased; nor is it easy to imagine how a cogent demonstration of this could possibly proceed. (The fact that metaphysical positions have *assumed* this position without demonstration is scarcely a recommendation for its adoption.) To adopt it would tend, in fact, to obscure a problem that does appear to be of considerable importance, namely, that concerned with *which* psychological states or processes can justifiably be said to be instances of bias, and which cannot.

In employing the terms 'subjective' and 'objective' we will, accordingly, be careful to make clear which of the alternative meanings of the two terms is at issue. In the controversies over the status of the social sciences it is clear that the questions have centered around whether unbiased investigation of (broadly speaking) psychological phenomena is possible, rather than around the absurd question of whether nonpsychological (the alternative meaning) states of knowledge are attainable. Thus, in coming to assess the charges against the social sciences we shall, in fact, be concerned with what sense it makes to speak of social science as being irremediably biased.

In the relevant sense of our discussion, 'objective' has, in fact, been used to apply to at least four different things: (1) the verisimilitude of ideas, i.e., the replicalike character of mental imagery, (2) the truth of statements, (3) the reliability of methodologies, and (4) the psychological disposition of an investigator to have, or believe, or employ the kinds of ideas, statements, or methodologies mentioned under 1, 2, or 3.

It is evident that 'unbiased' or 'objective,' in the sense of 4, is derived from the preceding three senses, and we shall, accordingly, confine our brief analyses to 1, 2, and 3 on the assumption that 4 would present no (relevant) special problems were 1, 2, and 3 to be satisfactorily clarified.

1. *'Objectivity' as a predicate of ideas.* The view that objectivity is to be found in a certain correspondence between our ideas—construed somewhat naively as mental imagery or picturizations—and those things of which they are ideas, has often been attributed to John Locke (however justifiably is not at issue here). Whatever may have been the precise nature of Locke's views, there can be little doubt that many people have held, and many continue to hold, that our mental picturizations in this sense are objective, insofar as they exactly resemble what they are "pictures" of. This is a sort of snapshot theory of objectivity.

However, despite the popularity of this man-in-the-street notion of objectivity, it has some formidable difficulties: (*a*) The sense of 'exact resemblance' that it involves is quite obscure. Are our mental images supposed to be as tall, heavy, dry, or smooth textured as those things of which they are mental images? If so, in what sense? If not, what is meant by 'resemblance'? It may be possible to overcome these difficulties and give satisfactory answers to such questions, but even the beginning of an attempt to do so reveals that the "snapshot" theory of objectivity is not nearly so straightforward or uncomplicated as it may initially have appeared. (*b*) It is *not* the case that all of our ideas of extraideational entities are picturizations. Not all of our mentation can by any means be construed as pictorial in character; and if this is true, what can be meant by 'resemblance' between our *nonpictorial* ideas and that of which they are ideas? The "snapshot" theory of objectivity provides us with no means for dealing with such problems. (*c*) Most crucial, perhaps, is the fatal defect in the fundamental assumption that underlies the entire position; for this view of objectivity seems to presuppose that we can in some mysterious way *directly* compare our ideas with something we would have to know 'nonideationally.' The very grammar of 'comparing' in this context entails *observing* or *perceiving* or *sensing* or *knowing*, etc., the things to be compared. But to do this for one of the pair as the position demands, without having any "mental contents"—to go *out of our minds*, so to speak, in just the sense the position appears to require—is to seek to fulfill a self-contradictory or nonsensical requirement. And the "snapshot" theory accordingly seems as obscure or self-inconsistent as is the criterion of objectivity it presupposes.

2. *'Objectivity' as truth.* The sense of the term 'true' (or 'false') throughout this book is, in general, that of the *semantic conception of truth*, which implies that 'true' and 'false' are construed as predicates that apply to linguistic entities, i.e., sentences (or in our slightly broader usage, statements). It follows that extralinguistic entities are neither true nor false—existence may be claimed or denied for such nonlinguistic entities but not, properly, truth or falsity. It is what we *say*

about extralinguistic entities, our accounts of them or descriptions of them, that are either true or false. Consequently, to identify objectivity with truth is to make 'objectivity' a predicate of statements. And indeed there does appear to be a well-entrenched usage of the term in which it is employed in just this sense. Thus, for example, when we speak of someone as giving "a factual, or objective, account" of something, we appear to be saying little more than that it is a true account.[3] This view of the nature of objectivity, unlike the preceding one, seems relatively unproblematical.

3. *'Objectivity' as a predicate of methods.* Predicating 'objectivity' of sentences by no means exhausts the well-entrenched uses to which the term is put; consider 'he adopted an objective mode of investigating the facts' or 'he proceeded to inquire in an objective manner' or 'he employed an objective method in investigating . . . ,' etc. Here, it seems obvious that the application of the term is not to sentences, but to means or methods of conducting inquiries. In terms of our present concern, this must be regarded as an application to the methodology, logic, or criteria of validation that we adopt in conducting inquiries. What is needed, accordingly, for this usage, is an analysis of just what is being asserted when we claim that one methodology is objective, or more objective than another.

In asserting that one method is more objective than another, we appear to be claiming that it is more *reliable* than that other. And the sense of 'reliability' involved would appear to be satisfied by the following criterion: Method A is more reliable than Method B if, and only if, its continued employment is less liable to error (i.e., is less likely to result in our continuing to believe, or coming to believe, false sentences). Correspondingly, we might say that a method was "maximally reliable" if, among all alternatives, it minimized the likelihood of error in this sense. Again correspondingly, we might say that a method was "absolutely reliable" if it made error impossible.

This account enables us to take explicit note of some generally useful characteristics involving the attribution of objectivity to methods. It can be seen at once that the demand that a method of *empirical* inquiry (i.e., inquiry into matters of fact) be absolutely reliable (absolutely objective) is self-contradictory; this is similar to the demand that a circle be squared or that a precise terminating decimal value be given for the number π. Empirical inquiry is, *logically*, not the kind of inquiry that can be undertaken in a manner to make error impossible. Next, among the various methodologies advocated in the course of intellectual history for the investigation of the universe, none has been shown to

[3] On such occasions we may sometimes be invoking the appropriate derivative sense 4 of objectivity, i.e., we may also be claiming that not only are the sentences of the account true, but that the account is not misleading in that it disposes us to believe certain other sentences that are true. Similarly, in claiming that an account is nonobjective we may be saying that it disposes us to believe certain other sentences that are false.

be more reliable than the method of science. This is due in part to science's insistence on *corrigibility*—the insistence that any hypothesis, however well-confirmed, may be susceptible to *disconfirmation* in the light of future investigation. The books, so to speak, are never closed on any hypothesis in the precise sense that evidence relevant to the confirmation or disconfirmation of it can never be exhausted. Accordingly, it is fair to say that if a hypothesis we accept is false, the continued application of scientific method to its investigation will increase the likelihood that we will be able to correct our error by coming upon evidence that disconfirms it. It is in this sense, of a systematically built-in mechanism of corrigibility, that the intellectual history of the species has presented man with no more reliable (i.e., in sense 3, no more objective) method of inquiry than that of science.

b) *The objectivity of social science.* Our survey of various relevant senses in which the terms 'objective' and 'subjective' (or 'nonobjective') have been used now places us in a better position to assess the specific charge that the social sciences fail in attaining objectivity. Patently, the charge must amount to an attribution of bias in social science if it is to be regarded as a nontrivial charge. At the same time we can dismiss the charge in the sense of 1 or 2 above as being clearly unwarranted— in the sense of 1 because, as we have seen, the sense of 'objectivity' it presupposes is itself too defective and obscure to be credited; in the sense of 2 because it comes to the claim that the social sciences are precluded from the acquistion of any true hypotheses or theories. This latter charge is obviously refuted by the fact that social scientists have in the past believed, and doubtless will continue to believe, *contradictory* hypotheses (i.e., hypotheses that contradict other hypotheses believed by social scientists). Of course we may not know, or we may not have good evidence for deciding, which of a contradictory pair of sentences is true; but it is logically necessary that one of every such pair should *be* true. Since there is no reason to believe that some social scientists will fail in the future to accept hypotheses that are the contradictories of hypotheses accepted by other social scientists (or indeed, by themselves in the past), we may reasonably conclude that social science has neither been nor will be precluded from the acquisition of some true hypotheses.

However, the charge of nonobjectivity is not likely to have been leveled in precisely the sense of 2—certainly not by any serious thinker who has been aware of its import as just outlined. In fact, we must seek the serious instances of the charge among those who have intended it in relation to 3.

From the point of view of methodology, then, the charge of nonobjectivity may be construed in either of at least two ways: (*a*) the scientific method is nonobjective and therefore its employment in the social sciences warrants the charge against them; (*b*) the social sciences must by their nature employ a less objective method of inquiry than the scientific method.

If we interpret the charge as being directed in general against the reliability of the scientific method itself, there again seem to be no decisive reasons for crediting the charge. In the light of what we have said above, the claim that the method of science is not *absolutely objective*, for example, would be seen to be defective as well as based on a misconstrual of the nature of empirical inquiry. But no alternative methodology has been shown to be more objective than—or even as objective as—the method of science. Indeed, there is good reason to believe that the method of science is maximally objective. Finally, it is clear that the charge against the scientific method in general does not place the social sciences in any more invidious a position than the non-social sciences; accordingly, it is difficult to take seriously any such arguments, which purport to be establishing a peculiarly nonobjective status for social science.

The alternative interpretation of the charge that social science is without methodological objectivity—and the last one we are to consider—takes a position in some ways diametrically opposed to the one just mentioned. It concedes, or at least does not question, the objectivity of the scientific method, but holds instead that the social sciences cannot use such an objective method; the social sciences must either eschew or supplement the use of the scientific method in such a fashion that the resulting methodology falls short of the degree of objectivity characteristic of the scientific method.

This argument is, in fact, close to those allegations (see section 13) concerning the impossibility of a social science that stem from a supposed complexity or other alleged peculiarity of social phenomena. Accordingly, we can perhaps do no better than to examine Max Weber's well-known espousal of this view, a view argued at least as persuasively by him as by anyone else who has come along since he wrote on the topic.

Weber offers a variety of arguments for his position on the irremediable (methodological) subjectivity of the social sciences, some of which were mentioned in the last part of section 13. But two further and closely related arguments deserve detailed consideration. These begin with premises about the character of social phenomena and the aim of social inquiry, and proceed to conclusions about the inadequacy of the scientific method to fulfill this aim, the need to supplement the scientific method by special methodological adjuncts peculiar to social science, and end with the claim that these special but indispensable adjuncts render social science methodologically nonobjective.

What (according to Weber and others) renders social phenomena idiosyncratic is the quality of *meaningfulness* that typically attaches to such phenomena. Moreover, according to proponents of this view, it is an essential aim of social inquiry to come to an understanding of the specific meaningfulness attaching to each such phenomenon studied. To appreciate the force of this kind of argument we must, at the outset, attempt to clarify the concept of meaningfulness. One of the chief difficulties involving this is that in English, as in several other natural languages, words like 'meaningful' and 'significant' and their cognates occur with a certain systematic ambiguity.

These particular words and their cognates can be used, first, in a *semantical (nonevaluational)* sense—a sense in which we are explicitly addressing ourselves to the semantical (i.e., referential or significatory) aspects of language itself. Thus, when we ask "What is the meaning of the word 'elephant'?" we need not be asking for an evaluation—in the sense of a judgment about importance—of the word 'elephant' or its referent. In the second place, there are many contexts in which our questions about the meanings of things are not, or not *merely*, inquiries concerning semantical (evaluationally neutral) characteristics. Rather, they are primarily questions about the importance or value those things may have. It is this sense of 'meaning' that is at stake when we ask "What is the meaning of (i.e., what is the importance of, or what are important consequences of) France's refusal to sign the test-ban treaty so far as the Atlantic Alliance is concerned?" or when we assert "The state visit of Greek royalty to England last year was an empty gesture—a gesture without meaning."

We are, then, confronted in these arguments with a key word that is systematically ambiguous; it behooves us therefore to distinguish carefully between the two versions of the arguments as determined by the two meanings of 'meaningful.' To facilitate the discussion we shall use the term 'meaning$_1$' (or 'significance$_1$') for indications of the semantical sense, and 'meaning$_2$' (or 'significance$_2$') for indications of the evaluational sense. In assessing the arguments we must keep the two senses distinct, even though it is not always clear that the parties to the controversy have succeeded in doing so.

Consider first the argument based upon the meaningfulness$_2$, or significance$_2$, of social phenomena. We may grant at once that not only do objects and acts that have value or importance come within the purview of social inquiry, but also that acts *of* valuing (whether or not such acts have value) are likewise suitable objects of investigation for the social scientist. The issue that arises is whether such phenomena necessitate a special methodology for their study. Is there any reason to believe that a hypothesis like (*a*) 'X is valued or judged to be important by Y' is *logically* impervious to validation through the scientific method?

It is crucial to notice here that this is an issue in the context of validation and not in the context of discovery—it is a question of method or logic or the rationale of validation, and not one of technique of investigation. Incidentally, the Weberian position cannot be construed as merely technological on pain of instant trivialization—it would become simply the uninteresting claim that different techniques need to be employed in different disciplines. On the other hand, from the methodological point of view, the arguments that purport to show that hypotheses like (*a*) are not amenable to the scientific method of validation, are singularly uncompelling. Generally speaking, these arguments are of two sorts, one being to the effect that value phenomena require that the inquirer himself make a value judgment in order to validate hypotheses concerning their occurrence or some characteristic they may have. The reason advanced to support this claim seems simply to be the presupposition that in order for us to determine, say, that X is regarded as important by Y, or that Y regards X as having some other valuationally relevant characteristic, it is necessary for us, through some empatic act, "to put ourselves in the place of" the evaluating subject of the inquiry. If we do not do this, the argument appears to claim, it will be impossible for us to tell (i.e., to validate the hypothesis) that X is valued, or to ascertain how it is valued.

The second argument, closely related to the first, holds that there is no sort of observable, or empirically testable, *behavior* whose occurrence is both necessary and sufficient for the applicability of any valuational predicates; and that, accordingly, it is impossible to employ the standard validational steps of the scientific method to test hypotheses about valuations. In terms of our discussions in Chapter 2, this amounts to the claim that valuational predicates that occur in social-science theories or hypotheses are not definable by any set of observation predicates, not even introspective or empathic ones.

This last contention, and others related to it, are among the most vexed problems in current analytical philosophy and it would be quite outside the province of this discussion to attempt to settle it and them here. But we do not have to settle these problems in order to reject both of the arguments just considered. For the scientific validation of the types of hypothesis involved is not dependent on the *synonymy* of valuational predicates with any set of observational (or introspective) ones. All that is required for scientific validation of the relevant hypothesis is that *some* observable state of affairs be a *likely concomitant* of the value phenomenon in question and not that any observable state of affairs be both a necessary and sufficient condition for it. To be sure, in taking the observable concomitant—or its absence—simply as evidence relevant to the hypothesis, we can never know with certainty whether the hypothesis is true or false; but certainty cannot attach to the results of *any* empirical inquiry, and our position of having to accept or reject a valuational hypothesis in the absence of absolutely conclusive evidence is simply the very condition of scientific inquiry. (Indeed, one suspects that it is the very urgency of some atavistic "quest for certainty" in empirical inquiry that has blinded otherwise perspicacious philosophers and scientists to this point.) At any rate, here we need neither accept the second argument that standard validational procedures are inapplicable to value phenomena nor, a fortiori, the stronger first argument that some substitute (empathylike) method is indispensable to their validation. It just *doesn't* take a fat cowherd to drive fat kine!

We have been examining the view that what has been called the meaning$_2$ of social phenomena necessitates a peculiar methodological divorce of social science from the rest of science. Though we have not couched the arguments at issue in just the terminology of Weber's own discussion, the arguments examined (or ones having substantially their import) do put in an appearance in one guise or another in his works on the objectivity of social science.

But Weber also seems at times to be arguing from the meaningfulness$_1$ (i.e., semantical meaningfulness) of phenomena to the same conclusion. And more recently, several extremely acute analytical philosophers, apparently under the influence of Wittgenstein's later writings, have also put forward subtle and profound arguments toward an even more radical (if closely related) conclusion. The work of Peter Winch (see bibliography) is especially challenging.

Winch (and doubtless Weber too) would hold that the concept of a social phenomenon or act must be coextensive with (i.e., refer to just the same things as) that of a meaningful$_1$ act. He holds that it is a definitory or essential characteristic of social acts that they should have meaning in what we have been calling the semantical (or significatory) sense of the term.[4] He explicates his use of 'meaningful' (i.e., our 'meaningful$_1$') by equating meaningful behavior with *rule-governed behavior*. He then contends that we must surely fail as students of the character of social phenomena unless we come to understand the meaning$_1$ of such phenomena. Yet, to do this we must understand what it is to behave in conformity with a rule or what it is to "follow a rule." In particular, we must understand what it is to follow the particular rule(s) governing the meaningful$_1$ phenomenon in question.

The explication given by Winch of what it is to follow a rule, is attributed by him to Wittgenstein. Winch tells us that to follow a rule is to act in such a manner that one's action commits one to, and is a sign of commitment to, some further act that it portends and whose nonrealization would presumably constitute a violation of the rule. Rule violation is indeed the key notion involved. We are said to know what it is to follow the rule (and thus, presumably, to "understand" the social phenomena involved) only if we know what would constitute a violation of it. Hence, we know the rule only if we can cogently make judgments of correctness or incorrectness about the act in question.

Having established this much (at least to his own ostensible satisfaction) Winch then raises the question of how an inquirer (or indeed anyone) can come to know or learn what it is to follow a rule, and thus come to know or learn the meaning$_1$ of any social phenomenon. This question brings us to the nub of the matter. For Winch's answer is that the method of science is *wholly irrelevant* to the acquisition of this kind of knowledge; consequently, the scientific method is held to be inappropriate in attempting to consummate the essential task of social science—namely, the task of gaining an understanding of mean-

---

[4] For a fuller-scale treatment of the method of science, and additional material relevant to the discussion above, see Chap. 3 in Wesley Salmon, *Logic*, and Carl Hempel, *Philosophy of Natural Science*, in the Prentice-Hall Foundations of Philosophy Series.

ingful$_1$ phenomena. It is, according to this view, at best misleading and ineffectual to employ the method used by the rest of the sciences in an area that belongs uniquely to social science. The method Winch claims actually to be appropriate is that of *philosophical analysis* (which for Winch is a task of learning the relevant rules). Sociology (in particular) is thus held by him to be a branch of philosophy rather than an empirical science. The kind of methodology Winch is advocating, would give us, in contrast to the scientific method, just the sort of understanding of the meaning$_1$ of a social act that the subject agent, i.e., the follower of the appropriate rule, himself has.

Now this is a complex argument, and it has ramifications for other areas of philosophy that again cannot appropriately be brought within the scope of this discussion. We are, however, fortunately in a position to assess its worth for our own context without having to explore these extraneous ramifications. Our discussion of the "reproductive fallacy" in section 13 makes it possible for us to treat Winch's complex argument with relative succinctness.

Suppose we were to grant both Winch's contention that all social phenomena are meaningful$_1$ phenomena and also that meaningful$_1$ phenomena are rule-governed phenomena. Even granting this much, Winch's argument seems to fail. Whatever plausibility it has stems from a disguised equivocation over the term 'understanding.' It is hard to cavil at the precept that a social scientist must gain an understanding of the phenomena he investigates, or at the apparent truism that a phenomenon is susceptible of being understood if, and only if, it is intelligible (i.e., understandable). But the next move in Winch's argument, a move that consists in adopting the precept that a meaningful phenomenon is not intelligible or understandable unless its meaning can be understood, makes a pivotal use of the equivocation.

For there are at least two senses of 'understanding' at issue, one of which warrants the application of the term only if the individual to whom it applies has had certain *direct* experiences of the subject matter being "understood." 'Understand,' in the other sense, does not have the occurrence of such experiences as a necessary condition. For example, with respect to the natural sciences it is generally agreed that a scientific understanding or knowledge of things or events of a given kind does not necessarily presuppose direct experience of such things or events. Indeed, as Winch himself points out, we have acquired the understanding appropriate in *natural* science when we have achieved, say, a causal explanation of the type of event being investigated.

Still, there have always been philosophers (Bergson and Whitehead are notable examples) who, while agreeing that causal or scientific explanations of physical phenomena are as much as can be understood by physical science, have nevertheless taken this very fact to be symptomatic of the deficiency or limitations of the scientific method— even as employed in physics. A typical claim maintains that science distorts (through abstraction from) physical reality. It is held, for example, that a scientific description of a tornado conveys in only a feeble, truncated manner what is, on the other hand, conveyed with overpowering richness and fullness by the direct experience of a tornado.

In light of our discussion in section 13, the shortcomings of this view should be clear. We need but to remember Einstein's remark that it is not the function of science to give the taste of the soup. It is the function of science to describe the world, not to reproduce it. Of course a description of a tornado is *not* the same thing as a tornado! And incidentally, the description does not "fail" to be a tornado on account of being incomplete, truncated, generalized, or abstract. Even if it were a "complete" description of a tornado—whatever that might be—it would still be a *description* of a tornado and not a tornado. Moreover, a description of a tornado no more *fails* to be a tornado than does a tornado fail to be a description.

How, in the end, does all of this bear on Winch's argument? The answer is that Winch's argument commits a rather subtle form of the "reproductive fallacy"—reminding ourselves of the character of the fallacy in the more neutral context of physical science (e.g., illustratively using tornados) allows us to discuss it more easily here. The claim that the only understanding appropriate to social science is one that consists of a reproduction of the conditions or states of affairs being studied, is logically the same as the claim that the only understanding appropriate to the investigation of tornados is that gained in the direct experience of tornados.

We can scarcely entertain the idea that the only kind of understanding at which we can aim in the investigation of tornados must come from the experiencing of tornados. Notice that in rejecting Winch's thesis, it is not necessary to deny that *some sort* of knowledge or understanding of, say, religion is gained in "playing" the "religious game," any more than it is necessary to deny that some sort of knowledge or understanding is gained in experiencing tornados. The point is that nothing whatever in such a concession implies that these direct understandings are either the only ones possible for the social scientist or that they are a substitute for a scientific understanding of social phenomena.[5]

Neither Weber's arguments nor the more contemporary but still rather Weberian arguments of Winch are decisive, then, in compelling the conclusion either that social science must fail of achieving the methodological objectivity of the rest of science or that social science must employ a radically distinct methodology.

[5] For a more detailed discussion of Winch's views and some of their ramifications, see in bibliography Brodbeck's "Meaning and Action."

FUNCTIONALISM

AND OTHER PROBLEMS

OF TELEOLOGICAL INQUIRY

5

15. The problems of functionalism

All of the social sciences have a common concern with purposive behavior and goal-directed, or *teleological*, systems. The phenomena we label '*social*' are almost invariably those we likewise call 'purposive.' As noted in Chapter 4, influential writers have argued that a quite separate methodology, a quite separate logic of justification, is appropriate to the social sciences. It seems clear that for many who hold this view—for convenience, let us call them *separatists*—the crucial fact about social phenomena is their pervasively teleological character.

In all of the social sciences, but most characteristically in sociology, anthropology, and political science, the problems of dealing with teleological phenomena arise most acutely in connection with what frequently is called *functionalism*, or the functionalist approach. Although initially we shall be dealing with teleological systems in general, the discussion below will also point up the need to distinguish functional phenomena from other teleological phenomena. The central question of this chapter will be most explicitly raised within the context of the analysis of problems of functionalism.

a) Functionalism and teleological inquiry. Not unexpectedly, what is sometimes called the problem of functionalism in contemporary social science, on reflection turns out to be a set of related problems, which in turn may be distinguished as two major and several minor problems. We shall, after identifying three of these, discuss one minor problem (by way of introduction) and then devote our attention to the two major issues.

Can we say clearly and with precision just what functionalism is? This constitutes the first major problem. Functionalism has been the topic of a discussion so voluminous and widespread in texts and treatises, that no one who has engaged in even a peripheral study of the social sciences can fail to have been confronted with references to it. Yet to be thus confronted is, unfortunately, usually to become convinced that the major task of saying clearly what constitutes functionalism still remains.

The second major problem becomes crucial once we have settled the first, for it concerns the merits of functionalism as a methodological proposal or tendency in social science. We must, in short, not only analyze functionalism, we must also assess its worth.

Let us now consider a minor problem: Is teleological explanation radically different from, and not reducible to, the kind of scientific explanation associated with nonteleological phenomena? Notice that to answer this question either affirmatively or negatively is also to take a methodological position. In the history of science there seems to have been no lack of proponents of each position, and although the controversies thus occasioned have by now probably lost some of their vitality and interest, a significant number of articulate and influential scholars continue to keep the issue alive by espousing the separatist view in the social sciences.

On a relatively uncomplicated level, it is not difficult to see that certain locutions—our commonsensical discourse about human behavior, for example—appear to lend support to the separatist position. Thus, in ordinary discourse, we frequently speak about behavior as though its occurrence is *caused* or *explained* by certain goals or ends. When we go on to identify these goals with certain future states of affairs (i.e., with events that have not yet occurred at the time of the behavior they are thought to explain or cause), we may find ourselves puzzled by this apparent anomaly into concluding that the realm of teleological phenomena is unique—effects seem to be temporally prior to their causes. Thus, we might be led to assert that Smith's goal, e.g., graduating with honors, explains or causes his present behavior, e.g., studying hard. But at the time of this assertion his graduation has not occurred. Accordingly, in identifying his goal with a future event and ascribing causal efficacy to it, some have been led to draw the paradoxical conclusion that future (i.e., nonexistent) events have causal efficacy.

It does not take much reflection to see the difficulty here, how we have been misled by certain ordinary modes of expression, and how we may resolve the puzzle by adopting a more rigorous or explicit manner of speech. We quickly realize, for example, that what was intended in our original assertion may be less misleadingly expressed by some such locution as 'Smith's present hard work is explained or caused by his (present) *desire* to achieve the goal of graduating with honors.'

Since the cause of Smith's behavior is identified with a state of affairs that does not occur subsequent to its effect, and since the same analysis will apply mutatis mutandis to any assertion of unrealized goals as causes, the puzzle is solved. We are not forced to conclude, despite the misleading possibilities of ordinary usage, that the realm of teleological events is inhabited by ghostlike states of affairs—nonexistent, yet somehow causally efficacious.

b) *Teleological discourse in science.* Of course, the example just considered is relatively trivial, so easily resolvable that we expect very few people actually to be puzzled, or at any rate puzzled long, by it. Another sort of example, slightly more technical and recalcitrant to analysis, however, has surely been influential upon separatists. This example is represented by "explanatory" statements such as the following:

1. The whiteness of the fur of polar bears is due to the fact that, in their natural habitat, this makes it difficult for them to be seen by their prey.
2. The purpose served by an increase of leucocytes in the blood stream during times of infection is that of guarding the body against attack by deleterious invading organisms.
3. Among the constituents of any human personality system will be a mechanism such as the propensity to forget material, the conscious entertainment of which would cause great pain. Without a mechanism such as *repression*, for example, the personality system might well give way under the strain of conflicts too painful to be long tolerated.
4. The persistence of type-X burial customs in society Y is explained not by the manifest functions or purposes attributed to them by the members of that society, but rather by their latent function: shoring up the members' feelings of group solidarity and hence improving morale in the face of the terrors death inevitably inspires in most humans.

All of these examples are ones that might occur in such technical contexts as textbooks and scientific treatises. All of them refer either explicitly or implicitly to *functions* or *purposes* and, accordingly, have the kind of subject matter we have been classifying as teleological. But these statements differ from the one first considered; they do not seem to be puzzling in the same way, and they seem to make no overt reference to nonexistent things as causes of existent ones.

Nevertheless, the statements do become a source of methodological problems when they (or examples like them) are construed as explanations different in kind from those given in the nonbehavioral sciences, and as the only sort of explanations appropriate to teleological phenomena. Since it is precisely in this fashion that the methodological separatists do view them, it is not surprising that statements of this sort have been taken (by all parties to the dispute) as a challenge to the analytical acumen of scientists and philosophers who do not share the separatist view.

What is required to meet the challenge is an analysis that reveals these problematical locutions to be similar to corresponding locutions in nonteleological contexts—similar in the precise sense that the methodology associated with their use need not differ from the methodology associated with use of the nonteleological locutions of science.

The strategy pursued in such philosophical analysis resembles that employed above in analyzing Smith's goal. Here, too, the analysis must show that the import of the problematical locutions can be expressed by some set of statements which are (in these contexts) scientifically or technically equivalent to the problematical one, but which do not furnish grounds for the separatist position. When successful, such analyses reveal the problematical locutions to be innocuous from the nonseparatist point of view. For in providing an equivalent alternative that is methodologically innocuous, the philosophical analyst shows that the problematical locution is merely a way of speaking—an elliptical way of making an assertion which we may at our discretion alternatively formulate so that no part of its scientific import will be lost, changed, or added to, but which no longer lends support to the separatist position.

Let us examine the four examples once more for the light they may throw on several related puzzles. The suggestion of teleological agencies or characteristics imparted by the wording of Example 1 is oblique, but nevertheless strong enough to occasion the claim that it illustrates a type of explanation radically different from ones appropriate to nonteleological phenomena. As construed by the separatists, the whiteness of polar bear fur is taken to be explained by an "end" or "purpose" which that whiteness serves—here, presumably, its conferring a comparative invisibility from prey.

With the contributions of Charles Darwin, nonseparatist analyses of these statements have become routine. In taking the statement explanatorily, the nonseparatist will construe it to be severely elliptical. He offers an alternative that (*a*) is scientifically or technically equivalent to the original ellipsis and (*b*) involves a methodology of explanation not different from that appropriate to nonteleological phenomena. The analysis in fact draws upon the conceptual resources provided by the theory of biological evolution. By making use of such concepts as *mutation* and *natural selection*, the analysis shows that statements linking the likelihood of the persistence, or survival, of species such as polar bears (in polar environments) with enhanced ability to carry on predatory activities that white fur contributes, are able to provide a standard explanation for the phenomenon in question. A fully explicit alternative might thus tell us that (in snowy regions) the occurrence of white fur as a mutation will increase the probability of survival of those animals in which it does occur because it increases their probability of successful food-gathering. The increase in the probability of survival of such mutant animals in turn increases the probability that they will live long enough to reproduce and transmit the mutant gene(s). In successive generations, the proportion in the total species of members exhibiting the successful mutation is likely to rise (on the assumption, say, that matings occur randomly in any given neighborhood) until white fur occurs virtually without exception in the species.

In sum, an alternative and explicit formulation of the explanation of white fur in polar bears could be given which does involve the relative invisibility to prey conferred by that characteristic, but which makes reference only to the nonteleological mechanisms of evolutionary theory.

The second type of example (of which a myriad of instances occurs in the literature and discourse of biologists) is especially germane to the topic of functionalism since studying it allows us to become acquainted with the notion of a teleological system. Nonseparatists have, in fact, often furnished analyses of examples of this kind by explicitly treating them as elliptical references to *systems* of entities, not merely as an allusion to an effect of the event in question. That is, the analysis is not taken simply to be of the type, "An effect of an increase of leucocytes in the blood stream is. . . ." Rather, analyses that make some explanatory allusion, however oblique, to the existence of a complex organization or system are furnished. The causally related events of the example (e.g., the effects of the presence of leucocytes) are, according to this view, some, but by no means all, of the constituents of a complex system.

Note that according to this kind of nonseparatist analysis, the presence of teleological language (e.g., 'purpose') in the original example is taken not as an atavistic bit of rhetoric, but rather, as an indication (whose dispensability thereby becomes a more complex problem) of the fact that the statement is about a *teleological system*. Construed in this way, the nonseparatist analysis of statements like 2 must then, to be innocuous, finally result in a nonseparatist explication of the concept of 'teleological system' itself.

In section 16 we shall place the nonseparatist analysis of teleological systems under close scrutiny. Before doing so, however, it would be well to notice how the treatment of this second of our four example-locutions has now brought us to a dividing point of some theoretical importance. The nonseparatist's simple treatment of Example 1 showed merely the direct eliminability in scientific discourse of certain references to purpose; this treatment does not involve any reference to systems. But the treatment of 2, 3, and 4 involves us not only in a reference to systems, but in an essential reference to teleological systems.

In any case, it is especially important to notice that the nonseparatist position by no means involves either a denial that there are such things as purposes, or a denial that the term 'purpose' may come to figure essentially in some scientific theories and explanations. Indeed, some phenomena for which analyses could be forthcoming might very well *be* teleological systems *of* human purposes. In such cases there may be no question of the indispensability of locutions such as 'purpose,' 'goal,' or 'end.' In sum, the social scientist may have to cope not only with examples in which there are, ostensibly, references to the purposes of obviously nonpurposive entities, but also with examples such as 3 and 4, which refer to systems containing constituents that undeniably *are* purposive entities: human beings and their purposive behavior.

Of course, not all systems of teleological entities need be teleological systems, just as not all teleological systems need be systems of teleological entities. This last is merely to point out that not all systems, properly characterizable as being goal directed, need have constituents or components that in turn are themselves goal directed.

However, the systems that do concern the social scientist are for the most part, teleological systems *of* teleological entities. And to these complex phenomena a discussion of the nature of teleological systems —a discussion broad enough to encompass the analyses of 2, 3, and 4— will provide us, independently of whether their constituents are teleological, with an appropriate introduction.

In this section we have been led gradually from a consideration of the solution of a minor problem concerning teleological locutions in ordinary discourse, to the threshold of certain major problems about teleological systems. Our ultimate aims in this chapter are to come to an understanding of the functionalist orientation in social science and to assess its merits as an orientation. But to achieve these aims we shall have to inquire by stages first into the nature of systems, then into the nature of both *teleological* and *functional* systems, and finally, into the uses of these concepts in *functional explanations*.

6. Extralinguistic systems

In chapters 2, 3, and 4 we were concerned mainly with those contexts of social science and philosophy in which the term 'system' is applied to sets of linguistic entities, our chief use of the word 'system' applying to *formulations* of various kinds that are used for descriptive or conceptual-organizational purposes in science. Our present business, however, is with certain *extralinguistic* entities, which, in fact, might be described or referred to by such formulations. We shall now discuss *extralinguistic systems*, and in the ensuing discussion unless otherwise specified, the term 'system' should be construed as referring to systematically related entities that are not necessarily linguistic.

Let us begin by making somewhat more explicit the relevant sense in which the term 'system' is to be used in these contexts. To this end, we may take a familiar (but for present purposes, greatly simplified) account of a familiar system, which is not, by the way, teleological: the solar system.

A scientific account of a system must include at least the following.

1. an identification of the *components* or elements of the system
2. a specification of the aspects or characteristics of the components, relative to which descriptions of the *states* of the system are to be provided
3. a specification of the set of *laws* in conformity with which states of the system succeed or precede each other, or with which elements of the system interact as regards the characteristics specified in 2

With respect to the solar system, our actual scientific knowledge is now such that we can fulfill these three conditions without great difficulty. We fulfill 1 by identifying Sol and its nine major planets as the components or elements of our system. Out of the immense numbers of characteristics or properties possessed by each of these elements, we choose two in terms of which to couch our descriptions of the solar system's states, namely, the momentum and location of each of the elements at any given time *t*.

This choice has the consequence of coordinating with each element of the system a pair of sentences (more strictly, a pair for each specifiable instant of time), one of which describes the momentum, the other, the location, of that element. Accordingly, for any given time *t*, a description of the state of our entire ten-element system will be comprised of twenty sentences whose form may be represented as follows.

$$L(s,t) = l_1; M(s,t) = m_1$$
$$L(e,t) = l_2; M(e,t) = m_2$$
$$L(u,t) = l_3; M(u,t) = m_3$$

These expressions might be read, 'The location of Sol at time *t* is l_1,' 'The momentum of Earth at time *t* is m_2,' 'The location of Uranus at time *t* is l_3.' (Locations, times, and momenta may be designated numerically; thus, in actual state-descriptions, the lower case letters '*l*,' '*t*,' and '*m*' might be replaced by numerals, or sets of numerals.) As was indicated above, the complete set of twenty sentences for time *t* will be called a *state-description*.

Momentum and location are our *variables of state*, or more briefly, *state-variables*. The actual number of state-variables required for any given system is not, of course, fixed at two and may well vary from system to system. In specifying location and momentum as state-variables, we fulfill the second of the three conditions necessary for providing a scientific account of a system.

The laws required in this example are the laws of celestial mechanics. They, together with some given state-description of the system (which we may call *an initial state-description*), allow us to deduce a description of the system's state (which we may call a *terminal state*) after a given time lapse (i.e., they allow us to predict the state-description for $t \pm \Delta t$). The process of furnishing such a deductive derivation will, of course, constitute either a prediction or an explanation of that terminal state, depending upon whether its date is or is not in the future of the employer of the deduction (see section 12).

The system we have just been outlining is standardly referred to as *deterministic*. It will be well to clear away some of the intellectual underbrush that has grown up around the notion of deterministic systems before proceeding to our scrutiny of teleological systems; for these latter will also turn out, for the most part, to be deterministic systems.

The primary application of the term 'deterministic' is to theories, and only derivatively does the term apply to extralinguistic systems. Perhaps the most important source of the confusion attending the use of 'deterministic' has been the failure to recognize that to call a theory deterministic is to say something about that theory's logical properties, broadly speaking, but nothing whatever about that theory's truth—and hence, nothing whatever about its degree of certitude. Moreover, to call a theory deterministic, without either explicitly or contextually providing some further information, makes no more sense than to say of someone that he is taller than. For just as a locution like "John Dewey is taller than" fails to make an assertion through, so to speak, failure to specify a requisite *relatum,* so too would the expression "Celestial mechanics is a deterministic theory" fail to make an assertion, unless some further information (which *is* usually supplied contextually) were also provided. This follows from the fact that a theory can be deterministic *only relative to some specific set of variables* (or properties of constituents) in systems to which they may apply. Thus, to say of a theory that it is deterministic is to say something like the following:

> To any given initial state-description of a system, and for a given time lapse, the theory coordinates one, and only one, terminal state-description (that is, from the laws of the theory and a state-description of the system at t, one and only one, state-description will be deducible for the system at $t' \neq t$).

Accordingly, if a theory is deterministic relative to some specific state-variables of a system, then, if at a given date that system is in an initial state S with respect to those variables, and the theory implies that it will be in state S' at a certain amount of time after (or before) that date, then the theory will likewise imply (and herein lies its deterministic character) that should the system ever again be in the state S, it will again, after (or before) the lapse of the same amount of time, be in the state S'.

This, perhaps is what many people have intended when, in connection with explicating the notion of determinism, they have said such things as 'same cause, same effect.'

The relational import of predicating 'deterministic' of a theory can readily be seen in connection with the example we have been using. For however deterministic celestial mechanics (that paradigm of "deterministic theories") may be with respect to the locations and moments of the constituents of the solar system, it is clearly not deterministic at all with respect to such characteristics as, say, their magnetic fields or their color or the level of intelligence of their inhabitants.

In the light of these considerations, it is easy to see that one must not confuse the predication of 'deterministic' with the claim that a theory is certain or that it predicts with certainty.

A theory is deterministic only if it has the logical characteristics described above; and it may have the characteristics that make it deterministic and still not be "certain." Indeed, deterministic theories not only fail to be certain, but they need not even be true. Many scientific theories, subsequently disconfirmed, and undoubtedly false (e.g., the humors theory of personality, or the caloric theory of heat), have been deterministic theories *par excellence.* The lesson to be learned here is that the extent to which a theory is probable or certain, is independent of whether its logical structure makes it a deterministic theory.

Having grasped the notion of a deterministic theory, the step to deterministic *systems* is not particularly troublesome; a system is deterministic, relative to some specified set of characteristics, only if there is a deterministic theory that predicts or explains its states relative to those characteristics.

17. Teleological
systems

Apparently, men have always interpreted a wide variety of the systematic phenomena they have observed as being teleological in character. For Aristotle and for the Thomists, as well as for most traditional theological positions, the universe as a whole comprised a teleological system. Hegel and the Marxists appear to hold human, or at least societal, history to be understandable only as a teleological (or goal-directed) system. These speculations, at least in their customary form, may today be dismissed as more or less unscientific. Nevertheless, even the most scientifically impeccable fields within the behavioral disciplines deal with some phenomena that are clearly teleological. Very few, if any, scientists or philosophers of science would now deny that some human beings sometimes behave in a purposive or goal-directed manner. (Many scientists, in fact, would agree that social groups, some nonhuman animals, and even some machines, behave in a purposive or goal-oriented manner.)

Our task here is first to clarify the import of saying that phenomena of this scientifically respectable kind may comprise a teleological system. Second, we must inquire into how teleological systems differ from nonteleological systems. And third, we must determine whether there is anything in the nature of teleological systems that substantiates the separatist view we have been scrutinizing all along.

Let us again begin with a simplified and abstracted example. Consider a system T that has only three components, u, v, and w, and three sets of metrical properties, P, Q, and R. (For present purposes, it does not matter what these measure.) Assume that P, Q, and R take on values denoted only by certain ranges of positive integers. Assume further that we have well-confirmed laws that tell us that things of type u may have P-properties in the range 30 to 70; that things of type v may have Q-properties in the range 1 to 10; and that things of type w may have R-properties in the range 20 to 60.

Now in addition to these characteristics of the components, consider some set of characteristics of the system T as a whole. Such characteristics may, for example, be mathematical or logical functions of characteristics of the system's constituents. (Thus, to revert to our nonteleological case as a clear example, the mass of the *whole* solar system will be a simple mathematical function of the masses of its constituents; or to take a slightly more interesting instance, the geometrical configuration of the whole solar system at any time will be determined by the location of each of its constituents at that time.) Let us call such characteristics of the *whole* system T, *E-states* of T. What we have thus far stipulated about our simple example of a teleological system may be summarized in the following table.

Constituents of the teleological system T	Variables of state in T	State-description sentences
u. . .	P. . .	$(P(u) = l)$ where $30 \leq l \leq 70$
v. . .	Q. . .	$(O(v) = m)$ where $1 \leq m \leq 10$
w. . .	R. . .	$(R(w) = n)$ where $20 \leq n \leq 60$

A state-description of T at any time t will consist of three sentences of the following form.

$$P(u, t) = l$$
$$Q(v, t) = m$$
$$R(w, t) = n$$

Given the limitations in the values that may be taken on by our three state-variables, it is apparent that the number of different, physically possible, state-descriptions will be a relatively small one (i.e., on the order of 20,000).

So far we have said virtually nothing about the *theory* of our teleological system. We shall remedy this by first delineating a subset (let us call it subset G) of the E-states of the *whole* system. Our choice of G may be made on any conventional basis—all that is required is that some criterion be provided by means of which the E-states that are to be counted as G may be distinguished from the E-states that are not G. Obviously, a concomitant of such a criterion is the division of the total set of E-states into two subclasses: G-states and non-G-states. Our theory of the system T, then, could be comprised of lawlike generalizations of the following sort.

1. generalizations that together with a given initial state-description, enable us to deduce that exactly one specific terminal state-description will hold at $t \pm \Delta t$
2. generalizations connecting E-states (i.e., lawlike statements from which, together with a description of an initial E-state, it is possible to deduce the description of some other E-states)
3. generalizations connecting state-descriptions with E-states
4. generalizations connecting state-descriptions with some specified subset, say G, of the E-states
5. generalizations connecting G-states with other G-states
6. generalizations connecting G-states with non-G-states

It should be noticed that so far our characterization of the system T does not differ methodologically from that of the solar system. The one apparent difference, our identification of the system's *E*-states and their division into *G* and non-*G*-states, is *not* methodologically . significant.

To show that this is so, it will suffice to illustrate how the non-teleological solar system is itself analyzable precisely as we have just analyzed *T*. We take as our *E*-states of the solar system the class of geometrical configurations into which it is possible for the ten components of the system to fall. Among these *E*-states two subclasses may be distinguished, namely, *E*-states in which all ten components fall on one *radial plane* from Sol as focus on the one hand, and those *E*-states in which this is not the case, on the other.

The *E*-states of the system that are in this sense radial are our *G*-states; the nonradial *E*-states are our non-*G*-states. The following diagrams may help to make this clear.

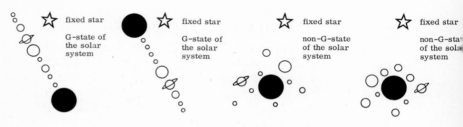

E-States of the Solar System

There will be for the solar system a great number of different *E*-states that are not *G*-states, as well as a great number that are. Accordingly, if our system *T* is to be regarded as teleological, while the solar system is not, then the basis for this distinction will not be found in the logic of the two systems (i.e., in formal properties of our characterizations of the two systems), for their logic is the same.

The actual basis for the distinction turns out to be not a matter of logic, but rather, a *matter of fact*. There happen, as a matter of fact, to be a large number of systems (on which the attention of human beings has come to be focused) which are such that their *G*-states may be distinguished as *preferred* states of those systems. ('Preferred' is a word that must be used with extreme caution, on pain of falling irretrievably into the very muddle our analysis is to clear up.) If such caution is to be properly exercised, it will be necessary to show that the use of the term 'preferred' here is merely a *façon de parler*—a convenience that (were we willing to employ some more rigorous, though pedestrian circumlocution) is wholly dispensable.

Demonstrating the dispensability of 'preferred' will occupy us shortly. For the time being, however, let us use it freely in order to facilitate exposition of the distinction between teleological and non-teleological systems. A teleological system, then, in contrast to a nonteleological system, has preferred states. To put it in another (equally metaphorical) way, it is one that displays preference for some of its E-states over others.

When we talk about actual systems, such preferred states are frequently referred to as the *goals* or *goal states* of the system. And such teleological systems, whether purely physical (e.g., servomechanical systems such as thermostats), physiological, psychological, or social, are frequently referred to as 'goal-oriented,' 'goal-directed,' or sometimes even 'purposive,' systems.

The question that immediately arises is how *do* teleological systems manifest their goal orientation or goal directedness, or purposiveness? The answer not only reveals the required dispensability of 'preferred,' but also reveals an important ambiguity in the usage of terms such as 'purposive' in the behavioral sciences.

Let us look again at the example furnished by system T. It will be remembered that its three state-variables, P, Q, and R, may take on integral values (indicated by l, m, and n) that range, respectively, between 30-70 ,1-10, and 20-60.

Further, let us identify the E-states of the system T as properties of the whole system, which the system exhibits as consequences of the system's components being in a state describable by any of its state-descriptions. This is to say that the theory of T will have some laws of type 3 mentioned on page 93, which specify that to every trio of values l, m, and n taken on by the state-variables P, Q, and R, there will be correlated some value e of the E-properties (properties of the system as a whole). Such laws as those belonging to type 3 may be quite varied, ranging from ones that appear to be amazingly simple to ones that appear immensely complex, depending on the character of the theory in which they occur.

In general, the value e of the E-properties of a system as a whole may be construed as some logical (e.g., mathematical) function of the state-variables of that system. For our system T this situation may be symbolically and succinctly expressed by the following equation.

$$e = f(P, Q, R)$$

The degree of complexity of the logical function f may be thought of as following directly from the degree of complexity of the type-3 law involved.

Now, let us take as the connecting logical function an example that is, no doubt, unrealistically simple. Let us say that the value of e is equal to twice the sum of the values of P, Q, and R. Thus, the abbreviated form would be expressed as follows.

$$e = 2(P + Q + R)$$

Given the ranges of integral values that it is possible for each of our state-variables to take on, it is easy to see that the sum of any trio of such values may vary between 51 $(30 + 1 + 20)$ and 140 $(70 + 10 + 60)$. Therefore, the values of e (twice these sums) for the whole system, on the basis of the function (lawlike statement), may vary between 102 as a minimum and 280 as a maximum.

We may now proceed to distinguish (on any basis) among all the possible values for E-states of T, some subset or other, and to categorize the members of that subset as the G-states of T. Our G-states of T could be taken as any range of *successive* values of e (e.g., the possible values of e between 200 and 210); or as a nonsuccessive set of the possible values of e (e.g., the set comprised of *just* the values 102 and 280); or as some single value of of all the possible values of e (e.g., the value of 200). We shall choose the last of these alternatives. Thus, T will be said to be in its G-state if its E-state value equals 200.

In our earlier terminology, to say or to accept the hypothesis that the G-state of T is a preferred state of T is to imply that T is a teleological system; alternative ways of saying this, such as the following, are frequently encountered: "T is goal oriented toward, or goal directed toward, G," "G is the goal of T," "T is purposively directed toward the attainment of the state G."

But how are we really to tell when a given G-state *is* a preferred state of the system? It is in deciding this question that the ambiguity of references to teleological phenomena in the behavioral sciences becomes apparent—an ambiguity that is not at all surprising considering the antecedent imprecision of the term 'preferred' (its vagueness *and* ambiguity) in the contexts of ordinary discourse from which we retrieve it. Accordingly, there is more than one plausible candidate for a criterion that distinguishes the requisite preferredness of a G-state in the technically precise sense we seek. Thus, depending upon which of these candidates we adopt, 'teleological system' or 'goal directedness,' etc., may refer to quite different things.

The general notion with which we must deal in speaking of preferredness might be crudely expressed by some such locution as "The system tends, or displays a greater tendency, to move toward some one state (or some one class of states), out of all its possible states—or, to stay in such a state if this has already been achieved." Our initial difficulty in analysis, then, seems to be due to the existence of more than one plausible way in which systems may be understood to display just such a tendency. Consider the following alternative analyses.

Analysis A. Let us take as an example a system like T, for which there is only a finite set of state-descriptions, and whose theory comprises type-3 laws (i.e., laws connecting each state-description with some E-state of the total system). It will follow that some E-states may be correlated by the laws with more of the possible state-descriptions than other E-states are. Thus, for example, there is only *one* state-description that, according to our type-3 law $(e = 2\,[P + Q + R])$, will yield the E-state $e = 102$, namely, the one in which each state-variable takes on its *minimal* value. (Similarly, there will be only one state-description yielding $e = 280$.) On the other hand, there will be more than 150 state-descriptions (i.e., more than 150 different combinations of the values of the state-variables) that in conformity with our type-3 law yield $e = 200$.

The E-state 200 is yielded by many different state-descriptions in contrast with the E-state 102, which is yielded by only one state-description.

Let us further refer to the number of the different state-descriptions that (in conformity with a system's type-3 laws) yield a given E-state as "the s-number" of that E-state. Thus, the s-number of the E-state 102 in our system T is 1 (because only one state-description will yield 102).

$$s\,(e = 102) = 1$$

On the other hand, the s-number of '$e = 200$,' is $|155$.

$$s\,(e = 200) = 155$$

Employing this analysis, we can now say precisely what is meant by 'preferredness' used in connection with such simplified systems as T. To say that system T displays a *preference for* the state E_1 over the state E_2 could be construed as the quite precise assertion that the s-number of E_1 is greater than the s-number of E_2 (i.e., out of all of the possible combinations of values of the state-variables, there are more combinations in this system yielding E_1 than there are yielding E_2). More to the point of our discussion, to say that out of all the possible E-states of T there is some *one* state (or some *one* set of states) G that is the goal of T, or toward which T is goal directed, would according to this analysis, be to say that G was that E-state (or set of E-states) whose s-number is maximal.

In similar fashion, we might even arrive at a plausible way of comparing different systems with respect to their goal directedness. For instance, a system T' might be said to be more highly goal directed to its goal G' than some other system T'' is directed toward *its* goal G'', only if the s-number of G' in T' represented a higher proportion of the possible state-descriptions of T' than did the s-number of G'' of the possible state-descriptions of T''.

Before concluding this analysis concerning a system's displays of preference, we may note explicitly that the analysis does appear to accomplish the task outlined earlier. It, together with the previous consideration of systems, appears to show us how scientific assertions we may wish to make about preference behavior of teleological systems may be made in a vocabulary and manner no different from the one required for nonteleological systems (i.e., vocabulary containing only such terms as 'state-description,' 'E-state,' 'G subset of the system's E-states,' 's-number,' etc.).

Analysis B. But the analysis given above of *preferredness* in teleological systems is not the only one available. Indeed, if it is not already apparent, a little reflection will doubtless show that that analysis may have some grave deficiencies for teleological systems that happen to be operating under somewhat different types of law from the system just outlined.

In particular, it might be argued that Analysis A would do very well for many systems if the "antecedent probability" of the occurrence of each state-description of a system were, in fact, equal to the "antecedent probability" of the occurrence of any other state-description. This being the case, the analysis given *would* tell us toward which of its *E*-states a system "tends." However, since there are very few (if any) teleological systems that warrant this "assumption of equiprobability," the analysis may be rejected as not fully adequate. For instance, it might reasonably be claimed that this inadequacy is glaringly highlighted for all those cases in which (whatever initial state of a teleological system is given) the probability is as a matter of fact very high that the system will eventuate in an *E*-state E_1 where E_1 has less than the maximal *s*-number.

If this is so, we might properly want to say that the system is goal oriented toward E_1 and not toward the maximally *s*-numbered *E*-state. Since the explication of 'preferredness' given in Analysis A would necessitate our always judging the maximally *s*-numbered *E*-state to be the goal state of the system, the cogency of that explication becomes dubious.

The apparent plausibility of Analysis A was, no doubt, derived from an implicit inference—namely, that since every state (described by each of the possible state-descriptions) is equiprobable, the system is, therefore, most likely to be in a maximally *s*-numbered *E*-state, and consequently, the system may be properly interpreted as "tending toward," or "displaying greater preference for," that *E*-state.

However, this inference is defective on a number of counts, the most important of which for present purposes is, as is perhaps already obvious, the dubiousness of the assumption of equiprobability associated with state-descriptions.

How might an alternative analysis remedy the difficulty? Let us again employ our example-system *T*. Suppose that the theory of *T* tells us there is a high probability that the system's variables of state will remain at their minimum values once these have been achieved. Suppose, also, that given any initial state-description with state-variables not at minimum (and hence, with an *E*-state value greater than 102), then, with high probability, any (later) *terminal* state will have an *E*-state value *e'*, where *e* is greater than *e'*. This assertion might also be put by saying that the theory contains a law, say, *L* whose import can be rendered as follows.

If $E\ (T, t) = e$, then with high probability $E'\ (T, t + \Delta t) = e'$;
and if $e \neq 102$, then $e > e'$.

In other words, unless the E-state of T is already at a minimum, successive states of the system will receive smaller values until the minimum E-state is realized. If our system T is correctly described by such a theory, then, even though the E-state of 102 would have (as it does) the *minimal* s-number associated with it, it might still properly be called a goal state of the system.

This counterexample to our first analysis not only shows certain defficiencies in that analysis but it also suggests an alternative way of explicating 'preferredness.' Taking our teleological system T again, and referring to its E-state, $e = 200$, we can begin our alternative analysis by raising the question—one that might, of course, be raised about any of T's E-states—'To what extent, if at all, is T goal directed toward the achievement of $e = 200$?' (Our task now is to determine whether we can give an explication of, and an answer to, such a question, that will be satisfactory from the nonseparatist viewpoint and yet will avoid the apparent defects of Analysis A.)

It will be remembered from our discussion of the ranges of the state-variables P, Q, and R of T, and of the relationship of T's E-states to the values of these variables, that there are a number of possible combinations of values for the three variables that will take T "out" of the state $e = 200$, as well as a number of combinations that will bring T "into" that state. Consider, now, the following two cases.

Case 1. At time t_1, the values of the three state-variables P, Q, and R, which we may respectively represent by l_1, m_1, and n_1, sum to 100 so that T is in the E-state $e = 200$.

At time t_2, the value of P changes so that $l_2 \neq l_1$. Every time this happens, there will be associated with the variables Q and R some probability, p, such that p is the probability that the values m_2 and n_2 (which Q and R may take on at t_2) added to the value l_2, will again sum to 100. Clearly, this probability provides us with a measure of the system's tendency to display *compensatory* behavior for, or to compensate for changes in, its P-characteristics—changes that otherwise would take it "out" of the E-state 200. On the basis of such a probability index of the system's compensatory behavior we can describe the degree to which the system may be said to be goal directed toward the E-state $e = 200$.

In this analysis of locutions such as "To what degree is T goal directed toward $e = 200$?" it is important to note certain qualifications: First, the actual measure to be adopted for degree of goal directedness (let us use 'g' for this measure) may be derived as any one of a variety of different logical functions of the probability-value p.

Thus, we might simply equate g with some specific p found to be associated with some arbitrary l_2. More plausibly, perhaps, a more complicated function of p might be taken as the determinant of g. For example, we might take g to be some function of both p and the value of the difference between l_1 and l_2; or again, we might take g to be a function of some p associated with the average of observed differences among changes in P from, say, its observed median or some other statistic.

Obviously, then, many different functions of p might be employed in deriving g, and our meaning for 'degree of goal directedness' would surely depend upon which such function was employed. From the point of view of the present discussion, however, whichever function was chosen would be immaterial; the choice of *any* of them would, without suffering from the patent defects of Analysis A, be compatible with the nonseparatist position.

While noting that our analysis does not *uniquely* specify a (law-like) determinant of g, there is a second qualification to keep in mind: this case actually provides us with an analysis only of what might be interpreted as the degree to which a system tends to maintain some E-state on the assumption that it is already in that E-state. This fact provides an indication that teleological systems may exhibit different *types* of teleology—different kinds of preference behavior.

Let us now consider our second case.

Case 2. At time t_1, the values $l_1 + m_1 + n_1$ sum to k, where $k \neq 100$, so that at t_1, T is *not* in $e = 200$. At time t_2, given that P takes on the value l_2, there will be associated with the variables Q and R, some probability, p, such that p is the probability that the values m_2 and n_2 will, together with l_2, sum to 100. By considerations corresponding to those given under Case 1, this probability-value furnishes us with a basis for determining a measure g^* of the degree to which T is goal directed toward the attainment of $e = 200$.

If the fact that our inquiry in both analyses A and B, which has eventuated in *several* nonseparatist explications of 'preferredness,' is taken as embarrassment for the nonseparatist position, it must nevertheless be acknowledged as embarrassment of the best kind: one of riches. It gives us a choice among several nonseparatist ways of using the concept in scientific theories.

Note, however, that the resulting analyses do not represent alternative explications of a single concept, *preferredness*. In fact, the existence of these alternatives indicates something that surely must come as no surprise—namely, that teleological systems may exhibit different kinds of preference behavior, and that the meaning of the term 'preference behavior,' in any context, must be qualified by the *kind* of preference behavior to which we are referring. Actually, we might not count a system as properly teleological unless it exhibited more than one type of preference behavior with respect to a goal state(s). The crucial point here is that whatever kind of preference behavior(s) we may be referring to in such contexts (whether it is of the kind explicated in Analysis A or of the kinds explicated or suggested in Analysis B), all of these analyses are compatible with the nonseparatist position.

8. Some lessons from the analysis of teleological systems

An important qualification to be remembered in connection with our treatment of teleological systems is the gross simplification of the particular abstract example, used for the purpose of meeting or illustrating only the basic methodological arguments relevant in this chapter. Consequently, the example must not be taken to resemble, except in barest outline structure, any *actual* system.

In fact, the significant differences between our example and "real" systems is not, as might be thought, found in the small number of state-variables or in the relatively narrow ranges of these variables. There may very well be actual systems with no more than three variables of equal or even narrower circumscribed range. Where the treatment of the example *does* radically depart from what would be involved in the study of actual systems, is in its abstraction from certain considerations of environment, and especially, theoretical complication.

a) *Environment.* In our illustrations of both the solar system and *T* we have chosen to abstract from reference to the *environment* (i.e., the remainder of the universe) of the systems that may causally impinge on them. This sort of abstraction has been appropriate because, again, those considerations of environment that are relevant involve equally teleological and nonteleological systems. Accordingly, such considerations would not be pertinent to our concern: the issue of whether there is a radical methodological distinction to be drawn between scientific inquiry into the two kinds of system. The reader, however, should keep in mind that the transition from our example to some actual system may involve our taking into account interactions between system and environment that are nowhere touched upon in our analysis.

b) *Theory.* The notorious difficulties of constructing viable theories of the phenomena studied by the behavioral sciences have obviously not been relevant to our discussion (though just as obviously, what the logical structure of those theories would be, were they constructed, has been crucial).

There is no need to labor the point concerning theory difficulties; these are evidenced by the scarcity of bodies of well-confirmed, well-articulated theory throughout all of the sciences of human behavior. Nevertheless, this melancholy consideration brings us to an issue of substance rather than methodology. It is salutary to remember that no amount of methodological clarity or rigor or sophistication, however helpful or needed, will suffice for the tasks of description, explanation, and prediction. Accomplishing these tasks is the ineluctable province of substantive *theory* in science.

When invidious comparisons are made between the social and the nonsocial sciences, the basis for pejorative judgments of the social sciences is not, in fact, to be found in methodology. On the whole, social scientists today seem at least as methodologically aware and sophisticated as physical scientists. Nor should the basis of such judgments against the behavioral sciences be sought in the availability of observational data—the amount of reliable data now available to behavioral scientists is staggering. Clearly, much more is available than can be digested. Instead, the basis of such a pejorative judgment rests precisely on the existence of well-articulated, well-confirmed, comprehensive bodies of theory in the nonsocial sciences in contrast to the few such "respectable" theories in the social sciences.

If the above remarks are warranted, the fact that actual examples of the scientific treatment of teleological systems in the social sciences are rare and immensely difficult to achieve should come as no surprise to anyone seeking an example of a full *substantive* application of our analyses of teleological systems to an actual system.

Beyond the fairly well-known difficulty attending the transition from our example to a "real" case, two additional (more minor) matters of substance should be noted.

It has been irrelevant to the purposes of our analysis to specify either the nature of the elements that make up our illustrative teleological system or the mechanism or processes that are causally efficacious in our system's changes of state. Accordingly, our system may serve equally well as a skeleton outline for any type of teleological system. It will serve in this fashion for systems such as the human body's digestive (or respiratory or circulatory or thermal) system, in which case the mechanisms for change in state would be physiochemical in nature; but it can also serve as the outline of a personality system with the system's elements being construed in, say, Freudian terms as an individual's *id*, *ego*, and *superego*. In this latter case, the mechanisms of changes of state would be psychological. Indeed, our example might serve equally well as the skeleton outline of a system of human beings, social groups, or social institutions—in which cases the mechanisms of changes of state would be, broadly speaking, sociological.

To say that the mechanism of changes of state are physiochemical or psychological or sociological, is simply to say that the laws describing those changes are themselves physiochemical, psychological, or sociological (i.e., they are laws that may, respectively, contain terms such as 'glucose,' 'reaction formation,' or 'socialization'). And to say this much is to assert that if the transition is to be made from our example system to an actual one (if the skeleton is to be fleshed out) it will likely be necessary to add and incorporate many complicated hypotheses or laws into the theory of the actual systems.

These remarks also highlight the fact that a system, actual or mythical, will be teleological (or will fail to be teleological) independently of whether its *elements* are physical, chemical, biological, psychological, or social, and consequently, independently of into which of these categories its mechanisms of changes of state fall.

The final matter of theoretical substance (which claims attention in considering a possible transition from our didactic illustration to actuality) involves our use of metrical variables of state. In our system T the properties P, Q, and R of the elements, and the relevant property

E of the total system, were (solely out of considerations of convenience and clarity) taken to be metrical properties. But it should be understood that the assumption of metricization is nowhere necessary to the main points of our analyses or the arguments to which they were addressed. It is perfectly possible for the theory of an actual system to eschew such metrical assumptions. Thus, the relevant properties of the elements of our example system or of an actual system might be referred to by such nonmetricized predicates as 'dry' and 'not dry,' 'circuit-closed' and 'circuit-open,' 'fixated' and 'not fixated,' 'sacred' and 'secular,' 'on the gold standard' and 'not on the gold standard,' or the like. Not only would the rationale of our analysis be unaffected by the use of nonmetrical state-properties or variables, and not only would it be perfectly possible for the theory of some actual system to be nonmetrically couched, but also it should be patent that the use of nonmetrical rather than metrical properties in theories need not constitute any lapse in rigor or accuracy in such theories. To be sure, the use of metrical variables allows us to bring into play well-explored deductive operations of great power and scope; but to confound such characteristics as the power or scope of a theory with the rigor or accuracy of that theory is simply to confuse aspects of the uses of mathematics in empirical science.

19. Functional systems

Our study of teleological systems will help us to analyze *functional systems*, which are types, or special cases, of these.

The literature of cultural or social anthropology, perhaps more than any other literature, evidences the great influence that functionalism has had on social scientists. For present purposes, we must first note that although references to functionalism or to functions do not always involve overt reference to functional systems, nevertheless, an examination of typical contexts shows that the reference to such systems *is* genuine and virtually universal—however hidden, implicit, or elliptically rendered they may be by the usual functionalist locutions. The degree to which such reference is disguised will, of course, vary from context to context and author to author. Pausing to note some specific examples of this implicit reference to a total system may help to orient the reader.

Clyde Kluckhohn generalizes as follows (see bibliography for the work cited, p. 28; my italics).

> Any cultural practice must be functional or it will disappear before long. That is, it must somehow *contribute to the survival of the society* or to the *adjustment* of the individual.

One chapter later in the same work (pp. 53-56), his involvement with a system, while still there, is not nearly so overt.

> Let us take the example of the Ghost Dance cult among the Sioux Indians sixty years ago when they were beset on all sides by the White Man. The more general features of this predominantly native religion can probably be explained in functional terms.

Among the social scientists who have profoundly influenced the character of functionalism, perhaps the most influential have been Malinowski, Radcliffe-Brown, and Merton. And among the works of these men it is not difficult to find assertions that demonstrate their awareness of the *systemic* aspect of discussions of functions. We find their substantiating remarks conveniently brought together and quoted in Merton's own important work on functionalism (see in bibliography; Chap. 1). The citation by Merton (pp. 25-26) of a remark of Radcliffe-Brown's surely makes clear just such an awareness.

> The function of a particular social usage is the contribution it makes to the total social life as the functioning of the total social system.

In the same chapter (p. 22), Merton provides us with a relevant quotation from Malinowski, citing a characterization in which Malinowski says the following of functional theory.

> It aims at the explanation of anthropological facts at all levels of their development by their function, by the part which they play within the integral system of culture, by the manner in which they are related to each other within the system.

As a final example, Merton himself shows a similar awareness (Chap. 1, p. 52) when he tells us:

> Embedded in every functional analysis is some conception, tacit or expressed, of the functional requirements of the system under observation.

Such citations suffice to indicate that our immediate concern (namely, to determine what, precisely, constitutes a functional *system*) is appropriate in any attempt to shed light on the nature of functionalism.[1]

a) A functional system from the literature. The clue that governs our analysis might actually be taken from any of a number of passages that are similar in their argumentative structure to the following paradigm from Malinowski (see in bibliography his *Magic, Science, and Religion*, pp. 52-53).

---

[1] It should be clear that the analysis of 'functional system,' given below, is not primarily intended as a critique of what Merton calls the 'prevailing postulates' of functionalism (see p. 25 of his work). Merton himself has shown the defectiveness of these postulates (which sum up many of the popular and erroneous views about the topic); and though the analysis of *functional systems* may also be used to substantiate the dubiousness of those "postulates," this is not its primary aim. Indeed, what we are now concerned with is the fact that the reference to functions *does* entail reference to functional *systems*, and that, regardless of whether the three postulates Merton scrutinizes are acceptable, the clarification of 'functional system' would still remain a desideratum.

The ritual despair, the obsequies, the acts of mourning, express the emotion of the bereaved and the loss of the whole group. They endorse and they duplicate the natural feelings of the survivors; they create a social event out of a natural fact. Yet, though in the acts of mourning, in the mimic despair of wailing, in the treatment of the corpse and in its disposal, nothing ulterior is achieved, these acts fulfill an important function and possess a considerable value for primitive culture.

What is this function? . . .

The death of a man or woman in a primitive group, consisting of a limited number of individuals, is an event of no mean importance. The nearest relatives and friends are disturbed to the depth of their emotional life. A small community bereft of a member, especially if he be important, is severly mutilated. The whole event breaks the normal course of life and shakes the moral foundations of society. The strong tendency on which we have insisted in the above description: to give way to fear and horror, to abandon the corpse, to run away from the village, to destroy all the belongings of the dead one—all these impulses exist, and if given way to would be extremely dangerous, disintegrating the group, destroying the material foundations of primitive culture. Death in a primitive society is, therefore, much more than the removal of a member. By setting in motion one part of the deep forces of the instinct of self-preservation, it threatens the very cohesion and solidarity of the group, and upon this depends the organization of that society, its tradition, and finally the whole culture. For if primitive man yielded always to the disintegrating impulses of his reaction to death, the continuity of tradition and the existence of material civilization would be made impossible.[2]

The import of such passages may be loosely summarized as follows.

1. An item or element of a cultural system (e.g., an act or event such as ritual wailing) is distinguished.
2. In the context of the system it has a characteristic (such as "expressing the loss of the whole group").
3. The occurrence of this characteristic determines, in turn, some characteristic of the whole system (the shoring up of feelings of group cohesiveness and solidarity against the threat of panicked dispersion of the group members).
4. This latter characteristic is necessary for the maintenance of the system in some state(s) (such as that of "survival").

On the basis of this four-point summary, we can bring to bear the results already attained by our analysis of general teleological systems in order to distinguish that subset of teleological systems which may properly be called *functional*.

[2] © 1955 by George Braziller, Inc. Reprinted with permission of the publisher.

Suppose, then, we were to use our previously explored example of a teleological system, T, as a basis for our present analysis. What modifications or additions would now serve to distinguish T as a *functional system?*

In fact, only a very few modifications would be required. For if we distinguish among the possible E-states of T some state(s), let us call it (them) N, and if the theory of T contains two required types of law connecting certain state-descriptions with N—and N, in turn, with some G of the E-states—our system T may then serve as a skeleton outline of functional systems.

The passage from Malinowski and our summary make clear the types of law that our theory of T must provide. That passage makes clear that the property R (expressing group loss) characterizing some element w (ritual wailing), is to be construed as a *sufficient condition* for the occurrence of an N-state (group cohesion and solidarity)— which N-state is, in turn, a *necessary condition* for the occurrence (in this instance, the maintenance) of some goal state G (survival) of the system.

If a system and its theory have the above characteristics, the system may be construed as functional. Derivative locutions in which some specific cultural item, say, w' (or some specific property of w', say, R') is referred to as *having a function*, may now be understood as simply an elliptical assertion that they have the indicated place *in* some functional system. It is important to notice this interpretation because so-called "functional explanation" takes place all too often through the use of such locutions as '. . . because x has the function y . . .' without further clarification.

This would complete our analysis of functional systems except for the fact that even a superficial perusal of the social-science literature in which the concept 'function' and its cognates occur, shows plainly that several important usages do appear to differ markedly from the one just derived from the Malinowski paradigm. Frequently, for example, the context makes clear that the item (or property of the item) that is described as *having a function* is not considered a sufficient condition for the occurrence of the corresponding N-state but only a *statistically correlated* condition. It will be evident, however, that analyses of such alternative usages could as easily be given by referring to *statistical* laws rather than to sufficient-condition-nonstatistical laws. Consequently, whether the sense of 'function' intended is that w (or R) is a sufficient, a necessary, a necessary-and-sufficient, or a neither-necessary-nor-sufficient-but-merely-correlated, condition of N, our mode of analysis can handle such an intent by simply modifying its description of the logical structure of the kind of law that connects state-descriptions with N-states. Thus, a complete methodological investigation might yield not just one kind of functional system but a variety of kinds, all of which have the characteristic of being special cases (i.e., subtypes) of teleological systems in our already analyzed senses of this latter concept.[3]

One other use of 'function,' which deviates from the Malinowskian, may also be noted: The term is sometimes explicitly or implicitly used in such a way as to make it patent that the functional system involved is itself a component or a member subsystem of some more comprehensive social system that has already been contextually identified. Clearly, such uses will offer no special difficulties for our analysis. The only source of possible confusion would entail mistaking that functional system, which is the object of our analysis, with the more comprehensive system (which may or may not itself be a functional system) containing it.

As these remarks suggest, a given cultural item may be a component in more than one functional system. It follows that not only may it (or some property of it) be "functional *for*" some of the possible *E*-states of system *T* while failing to be "functional *for*" other *E*-states of that system, but also it may be "functional *for*" some *E*-state of one system *T* while being (or *failing* to be) "functional *for*" an *E*-state of another system, *T'*, of which it is also a component.

20. Functional explanation

If the analysis given of functional systems is correct, it forges the final link in the chain of argument this chapter has been constructing against the separatist position. For it demonstrates that, contrary to the separatist view, it is not necessary for the social scientist to make a radical methodological break with the nonsocial scientist. For example, anyone who now wished to take a separatist position could *not* cogently argue as follows: "However fruitful the methodology of the physical sciences has been in its area, the teleological or functional nature of social-science phenomena forces the social scientist to adopt a radically distinct methodology."

In sections 9-12 of this book, we have had frequent occasion to point out that explanation is an important aspect of scientific methodology. In the light of our remarks on explanation and our analyses of functional systems, it becomes feasible at last to rigorously assess what has sometimes been called *functional explanation*, or explanation by reference to function, in the social sciences.

Perhaps the strongest and most unguarded claims for the efficacy of explanations of cultural phenomena by reference to their functions

---

[3] What has been said about variations in the type of connection between state-descriptions and *N*-states also applies (mutatis mutandis) to the connection between *N*-states and *G*-states in functional systems. For some uses of 'function' are properly interpreted as entailing that *N* is a sufficient condition, or a "merely correlated" condition, of *G* rather than a necessary condition, as in the analysis of "Malinowskian functions." The structural modifications required for such deviations are easily discerned and readily enough describable, resulting in the addition of several more subtypes of functional system to any complete catalog. But these too will constitute subtypes of teleological systems.

occurred during the second and third decades of this century. At that time the controversy between historically oriented and functionally oriented anthropologists waxed most hotly. But while it is probably true, as Kluckhohn asserts (see in bibliography his cited work, p. 55), that the subject of this controversy in anthropological circles today 'is now almost universally regarded as a false issue,' it is nevertheless evident that current anthropological literature does abound in implicit or explicit claims of the achievement of explanation by reference to the functions served by cultural phenomena.

However, not a single one of the myriad claims in the anthropological literature can be accepted without serious qualification—not because it is, in principle, impossible to achieve functional explanation (indeed, part of the import of the preceding sections of this chapter has been to indicate how, *in principle*, such explanations could be given), but rather, because the achievement of functional explanation simply is too difficult, much more difficult than the claimants appear to have realized.[4] All too frequently these claims may be counted as at most containing some more or less accurate *descriptions*, rather than explanations, of specific phenomena, couched in or accompanied by a rhetoric that may be mistaken for explanations by the unwary.

Compare the magnitude and complexity of the material that would have to be presented if a functional explanation were really given, with what is actually given in articles and books purporting to vouchsafe functional explanations. To furnish a functional explanation of, say, the cultural item x, it would be necessary at least to carry out the following.

1. Specify x through some accurate description of it.
2. Specify the constituents comprising the functional system Y.
3. Show that x is one of the constituents of Y.
4. Specify the state-variables of Y.
5. Show that some state-properties are properties of x and of other constituents of Y, as well, so that state-descriptions can be given.
6. Specify precisely what would constitute the set of E-states for the total system.
7. Specify precisely an N subset of the E-states.
8. Specify precisely the G subset of the E-states.
9. Specify a set of state-descriptions of Y, some of which are temporally prior (or posterior) to the one in which x is characterized by the *relevant* property (i.e., the property that "makes it functional").

[4] A similar charge could also be leveled against many sociologists, psychologists, political scientists, and economists, if one were to judge by their frequent use of statements whose import is something like the following: 'The occurrence of item x in (the culture, political system, personality system, society, or economy) Y is explained by x serving the function z.' Clearly, such statements do not of themselves constitute *explanations*, however *heuristically* full of insight they may be.

10. (And most difficult of all) produce a body of well-articulated theory which, as the theory of Y, contains at least laws connecting: (*a*) antecedent state-descriptions with the state-description in which Y has the relevant property; (*b*) the state-description, in which Y has the relevant property, with the specified N-state(s) of the total system; (*c*) the N-state(s) of Y with the specified G-state(s) of Y.

It is patent that nothing like the fulfillment of this staggering task has been accomplished in many (if any) of the works in which, to date, social scientists purport to be giving functional explanations. To give a functional explanation of the occurrence of *x* (more precisely, to give a functional explanation of the occurrence of some characteristic of *x*) requires both that we explain the occurence of *x* and that we provide an analysis of how *x* functions in a functional system—i.e., give its relationship to the system's N- and G-states.

In contrast with what would be involved in the accomplishment of this difficult task, the actual achievement of, say, anthropologists who *claim* to have arrived at functional explanations of cultural items, is minuscule. The results produced to date must be seen to amount only (so far as explanation is concerned) to the articulation of some pre-scientific hunches or pious hopes that a functional explanation for the item in question *can* ultimately be given. However, the purport of these remarks will have been misunderstood if they are construed as finding fault with, say, anthropologists on the grounds that they have not been able to provide explanations of the phenomena they study. This is not at all what we are saying. *Substantive* ignorance is never a fault of a science—it is the very condition for the existence of science. What does constitute a particularly deadly scientific sin, however (and it is one by no means confined to social scientists), is *methodological* ignorance, which may mislead, stultify, or close off badly needed inquiry both to the exhibitor of that ignorance and to those who are influenced by him.

21. Functionalism　　Our attention has so far been focused mainly on the analysis of functional systems and functional explanation. Yet, any reading of the literature in which discussions of functionalism figure makes it seem that there is more to functionalism than what is encompassed by those two topics. In particular, one may find numerous references employing terms such as 'functional orientation,' 'the functionalist position,' or 'the functionalist approach.' To point out that what is intended by such expressions is not always clear, is to understate the case. But insofar as what is meant is something other than reference to functional explanation, or functional analysis of systems, these terms seem best understood to apply to topics in the context of discovery rather than in the context of validation.

This is especially true for those locutions that are either disguised or undisguised exhortations, say, to the anthropologist to be "functionally oriented in the field." Such exhortations, one supposes, should presumably be interpreted as advice to the scientist in the field to look for (or to be prepared and inclined to entertain hypotheses concerning) the existence of functional systems, and thus the occurrence of functional relationships among the objects of his research.

If we do construe exhortations to be "functionally oriented," or arguments *for* "functional orientation," as more or less disguised advice to the *scientist* to adopt a certain psychological "set" or attitude toward his objects of inquiry, then the major question posed at the very outset of this chapter concerning the worth of the functionalist approach can be answered only by assessing the *heuristic* worth of adopting such psychological "sets" or attitudes. How would one go about doing this?

Clearly, it is an empirical matter to assess just how efficacious the adoption by the scientist of some attitudes may be in the acquisition of fruitful hypotheses. What is empirically involved is the attempt to answer such questions as, "Will the adoption of Attitude A in Circumstance B by Scientist C *cause* C to acquire a fruitful hypothesis?" This question is not only empirical, it belongs to a specific discipline, namely, the sociology (or psychology) of science.

Unfortunately, neither the sociology nor the psychology of science is among our most advanced scientific disciplines. And there are at hand no reliable scientific answers to such questions. Thus, the status of this sense of our question, "What is the worth of functionalism?" must be acknowledged as moot, in default of the production of any scientifically supported answer. We have, however, improved our position by now being able to recognize what would be involved in answering it.

To be sure, were we to base our judgment on what is probably the opinion of a majority of cultural anthropologists, we would certainly conclude in favor of the heuristic usefulness of "functional orientation." And indeed, in the absence of any other clues, it is obviously sensible to adopt this basis of decision.

In our discussion of various aspects of functionalism we have omitted treatment of one especially interesting pair of concepts that has captured the attention of contemporary anthropologists, sociologists, and clinical psychologists alike: 'manifest function' and 'latent function.' Suppose we construe these concepts in conformance with Merton's widely adopted characterizations which read as follows (see in bibliography his work, p. 51).

> *Manifest functions* are those objective consequences contributing to the adjustment or adaptation of the system which are intended and recognized by participants in the system;
> *Latent functions*, correlatively, being those which are neither intended nor recognized.

So far as the methodological issues touched on by our analysis of the nature of functional systems and functional explanations are concerned, we may remark that the introduction of these two interesting concepts is, strictly speaking, *irrelevant*. For those analyses do not rest on any specific assumptions regarding the "intentions" or "recognitions" of the "participants" in functional systems. It makes no difference for the purposes of our analysis whether the item in question is manifestly or latently functional; though of course our analysis does not preclude making this discrimination. On the other hand, any discussion of the heuristic efficacy of the "functionalist approach" should surely include at least brief mention of this useful pair of concepts. Indeed, it is evidently a part of the advice frequently proferred by functionalists that the study of a culture should be approached with an alertness on the part of the researcher to the fact that cultural items may have "functional consequences" that are unintended and unrecognized by the members of the culture.

This, if our own prescientific hunches are correct, is, like any general admonition to be alert, probably good advice.

For

further

reading

Ackermann, R. J., *Simplicity and the Acceptability of Scientific Theories.* Doctoral dissertation, Michigan State University, 1960.

Black, Max, *Critical Thinking,* second edition. Englewood Cliffs, N. J.: Prentice-Hall, Inc., 1952.

Braithwaite, R. B., *Scientific Explanation.* London: Cambridge University Press, 1953.

Brodbeck, May, "Meaning and Action," *Philosophy of Science,* Vol. 30, No. 4 (October 1963).

———, "Models, Meaning, and Theories," *Symposium on Sociological Theory,* ed. L. Gross. Evanston: Row, Peterson & Co., 1959.

Churchman, C. W., "Why Measure?" in *Measurement: Definition and Theories,* ed. C. W. Churchman and P. Ratoosh. New York: John Wiley & Sons, Inc., 1959.

Cowling, Maurice, *The Nature and Limits of Political Science.* London: Cambridge University Press, 1963.

Goodman, Nelson, *Fact, Fiction, and Forecast.* Cambridge: Harvard University Press, 1955.

———, *The Structure of Appearance.* Cambridge: Harvard University Press, 1951.

———, "The Test of Simplicity," *Science,* CXXVIII (1958), 1064-69.

Grünbaum, Adolf, "Temporally-Asymmetrical Principles. . . . ," *Philosophy of Science,* Vol. 29, No. 2 (1962).

Hayek, F. A., *The Counter-Revolution of Science.* New York: Free Press of Glencoe, Inc., 1952.

Hempel, Carl, "Deductive-Nomological vs. Statistical Explanation," *Minnesota Studies in the Philosophy of Science,* Vol. III, ed. H. Feigl et al. Minneapolis: University of Minnesota Press, 1962.

———, *Fundamentals of Concept Formation in Empirical Science, International Encyclopedia of Unified Science,* Vol. II, No. 7. Chicago: University of Chicago Press, 1952.

———, "The Logic of Functional Analysis," in *Symposium on Sociological Theory,* ed. Llewellyn Gross. Evanston: Row, Peterson & Co., 1959.

———, *Philosophy of Natural Science.* Prentice-Hall Foundations of Philosophy Series, 1966.

———, "Problems of Concept and Theory Formation in the Social Sciences," in *Science, Language and Human Rights.* Philadelphia: University of Pennsylvania Press, 1952.

———, "The Theoretician's Dilemma," *Concepts, Theories, and the Mind-Body Problem, Minnesota Studies in the Philosophy of Science,* Vol. II. Minneapolis: University of Minnesota Press, 1958.

Hempel, Carl, and Paul Oppenheim, "Studies in the Logic of Explanation," *Philosophy of Science*, Vol. XV (1948).

Kemeny, John G., "Two Measures of Simplicity," *The Journal of Philosophy*, Vol. LII (1955).

———, "The Use of Simplicity in Induction," *Philosophical Review*, Vol. LVII (1953).

Kluckhohn, Clyde, *Mirror for Man*. New York: Fawcett World Library, 1957. Premier edition.

Malinowski, B., "Culture," *Encyclopedia of Social Science*, Vol. IV (1931).

———, *Magic, Science, and Religion*. With an introduction by Robert Redfield. Garden City, N. Y.: Doubleday & Company, Inc., 1954.

Merton, Robert K., *Social Theory & Social Structure*, revised and enlarged edition. New York: Free Press of Glencoe, Inc., 1957.

Nagel, Ernest, *The Structure of Science*. New York: Harcourt, Brace & World, Inc., 1961.

Oakeshott, Michael, *Rationalism in Politics & Other Essays*. London: Methuen & Co., Ltd., 1962.

Parsons, Talcott, "Pattern Variables Revisited," *American Sociological Review*, XXV, No. 4, 467-83.

———, "The Point of View of the Author," in *The Social Theories of Talcott Parsons*, ed. Max Black. Englewood Cliffs, N. J.: Prentice-Hall, Inc., 1961.

Peters, R. S., *The Concept of Motivation*. London: Routledge & Kegan Paul, Ltd., 1958.

Radcliffe-Brown, A. R., "On the Concept of Function in Social Science," *American Anthropologist*, Vol. 37 (1935).

Robinson, Joan., *The Economics of Imperfect Competition*. London: Macmillan & Co., Ltd., 1933.

Rudner, Richard, "Comments on the Papers of Sellars, Salmon and Barker," in *Current Issues in the Philosophy of Science*, ed. H. Feigl and G. Maxwell. New York: Holt, Rinehart & Winston, Inc., 1961.

———, "An Introduction to Simplicity," *Philosophy of Science* Vol. 28, No. 2 (1961).

———, "Philosophy of Social Science," *Philosophy of Science*, Vol. 21, No. 2 (1954).

———, "The Scientist *Qua* Scientist Makes Value Judgments," *Philosophy of Science*, Vol. XX (1953).

Salmon, Wesley, *Logic*. Prentice-Hall Foundations of Philosophy Series, 1963.

Scheffler, I., "Prospects of a Modest Empiricism," *Review of Metaphysics*, Vol. X (1957).

Sellars, Wilfred, "The Language of Theories," in *Current Issues in the Philosophy of Science*, ed. H. Feigl and G. Maxwell. New York: Holt, Rinehart, & Winston, Inc., 1961.

Svenonius, Lars, "Definability and Simplicity," *Journal of Symbolic Logic*, Vol. XX (1955).

Weber, Max, " 'Objectivity' in Social Science and Social Policy," in *On the Methodology of the Social Sciences*, ed. and trans. E. A. Shils and H. A. Finch. New York: Free Press of Glencoe, Inc., 1949.

Winch, Peter, *The Idea of a Social Science*. New York: Humanities Press, 1958.

INDEX